MANAGING TALENT

OTHER ECONOMIST BOOKS

Guide to Analysing Companies
Guide to Business Modelling
Guide to Business Planning
Guide to Cash Management
Guide to Commodities
Guide to Decision Making
Guide to Economic Indicators
Guide to Emerging Markets
Guide to the European Union
Guide to Financial Management
Guide to Financial Markets
Guide to Hedge Funds
Guide to Investment Strategy
Guide to Management Ideas and Gurus
Guide to Managing Growth
Guide to Organisation Design
Guide to Project Management
Guide to Supply Chain Management
Numbers Guide
Style Guide

Book of Business Quotations
Book of Isms
Book of Obituaries
Brands and Branding
Business Consulting
Business Strategy
Buying Professional Services
Doing Business in China
Economics
Managing Uncertainty
Marketing
Marketing for Growth
Megachange – the world in 2050
Modern Warfare, Intelligence and Deterrence
Organisation Culture
Successful Strategy Execution
The World of Business

Directors: an A–Z Guide
Economics: an A–Z Guide
Investment: an A–Z Guide
Negotiation: an A–Z Guide

Pocket World in Figures

MANAGING TALENT

Recruiting, retaining and getting the most
from talented people

Marion Devine and Michel Syrett

THE ECONOMIST IN ASSOCIATION WITH
PROFILE BOOKS LTD

Published by Profile Books Ltd
3a Exmouth House
Pine Street
London EC1R 0JH
www.profilebooks.com

Typeset in EcoType by MacGuru Ltd
info@macguru.org.uk

Printed in Great Britain by Clays, Bungay, Suffolk

A CIP catalogue record for this book is available from the British Library

Hardback ISBN: 978 1 84668 573 6
Paperback ISBN: 978 1 84668 589 7
e-book ISBN: 978 1 84765 810 4

The paper this book is printed on is certified by the © 1996 Forest Stewardship Council A.C. (FSC). It is ancient-forest friendly. The printer holds FSC chain of custody SGS-COC-2061

FSC
www.fsc.org
MIX
Paper from
responsible sources
FSC® C018072

To our partners Stephen and Suzy

Contents

Preface

IN APPROACHING THE RESEARCH and development of this book, the authors were aware that there is already a large body of material on talent management on the market.

Yet in conducting the research to assess this material, a number of factors stood out. First, in the grand scheme of things, talent management is a relatively new concept. It has been around for only about a decade and as a study by Heidrick & Struggles, a global executive search firm, discovered, the creation of specifically focused talent development functions and managers is still in its early stage (see Chapter 1).

One consequence is that there is still no consensus about what talent management involves. As Angela Baron, formerly of the UK Chartered Institute of Personnel and Development, commented, it might or might not encompass a mixture of previously independent functions like graduate recruitment, performance management, career management and succession planning. Few of the new breed of talent managers are accountable directly to the chief executive or the senior executive team, and the level of integration between business and talent strategies is still patchy.

The other factor that stands out from interviewing people who are viewed as talented and/or have a track record of success in their chosen occupation is that there is a stark discontinuity between the agendas of the individual and that of the organisation. It can no longer be taken for granted by organisations that the individuals they mark out for systematic promotion and development are going to be willing pawns in the talent game created for them – not least because that often involves a high degree of mobility and a long-term commitment to extended career plans.

Furthermore, narrowly defined demarcations about who is inside or outside the talent pool often exclude the very people organisations need to attract and retain at a time of volatility and uncertainty: aspiring entrepreneurs, mavericks, outsiders and specialists who do not seek or want a career ladder to a top corporate position, and who desire independence and autonomy.

All this poses considerable challenges to the senior managers who seek to recruit, retain and benefit from the skills and insights of talented people. This book seeks to highlight the dilemmas they face and, through reference to organisations with a proven track record of success, define and outline some of the emerging solutions. It also includes a chapter aimed at "talented" people themselves and how they can best approach the talent game at a time when the rules are significantly in flux.

Marion Devine and Michel Syrett
January 2014

1 The war for talent

All of us know that the calibre of talent distinguishes great from good, winners from losers and adaptation from extinction. Having the right team playing on the field is the fundamental difference between victory and defeat.

Indra Nooyi, chairman and chief executive, PepsiCo

SOME 15 YEARS AGO, McKinsey & Company, a global management consulting firm, produced a now famous report called *The War for Talent*. It made the case that international companies needed to pay as much attention to how they managed their brightest employees as they did any other corporate resource. McKinsey declared that "better talent is worth fighting for" and predicted a world where the supply of talent would decrease while demand would rise. Companies would be locked in a constant and costly battle for the best people for the foreseeable future.

McKinsey's definition of talent went far beyond managerial or leadership skills:

> [Talent is] the sum of a person's abilities ... his or her intrinsic gifts, skills, knowledge, experience, intelligence, judgment, attitude, character and drive. It also includes his or her ability to learn.

In response to economic boom times between 1998 and 2001, many firms expanded rapidly and the battle to recruit and keep the best people well and truly began. The talent management function, as well as a burgeoning talent management industry, sprang up to identify, retain and develop high-flying individuals into a small, exclusive top tier of managers and leaders.

Despite several cycles of economic boom and bust, as well as the world's most severe economic crisis, the battle for talent continues. The competition for the best staff has broadened beyond senior leadership talent. Employers are struggling to recruit sufficient numbers of highly skilled people for a wide variety of managerial and specialist positions.

At the international level, talent shortages are more severe. During the past decade, an internationally mobile group of employees, who can pick and choose where they work, has emerged. As firms in emerging markets also begin competing in the global economy, these people are in ever-greater demand.

Singapore, for example, has embarked on an intensive recruitment programme for skilled foreign workers, with more liberal criteria for eligibility to work in the country. Some 90,000 now work in the city-state, the majority from the United States, the UK, France, Australia, Japan and South Korea.

The World Economic Forum predicts good times ahead for this internationally mobile group. In its 2012 report, *Stimulating Economies Through Fostering Talent Mobility*, which analyses the demand and supply of skilled workers in 22 countries and 12 industries, it comments:

> *The coming decades will present golden opportunities for well-educated people with critical expertise. So deep and widespread will be the talent gap that individuals willing to migrate will have unprecedented options.*

Annual surveys of employers worldwide between 2009 and 2013 by ManpowerGroup, a multinational human resources consulting firm, have shown steady rises in the number experiencing difficulties in recruiting skilled workers. The 2013 survey revealed that more than a third (35%) of nearly 40,000 employers worldwide are experiencing difficulties in filling vacancies. One in three employers in the United States is experiencing skills shortages; European employers are reporting similar shortages. Despite continued high unemployment in many European countries, especially those in the euro zone, more than one in four employers (26%) struggle to fill jobs because of talent shortages. Around three-quarters (73%) of responding firms say the main obstacle is a lack of people with the right level of experience, skills or knowledge to fill these positions.

Firms in the survey report the highest shortages since 2008, and over half (54%) believe that this will have a "high or medium impact" on their competitiveness. This is an increase from 42% in 2012. The jobs that are most difficult to fill include engineers, sales representatives, technicians, accounting and finance staff, managers and executives and information technology staff.

Jeffrey A. Joerres, ManpowerGroup's chairman and CEO comments:

> There is a collective awakening among the surveyed firms about the impact of talent shortages on their businesses. Globally, employers are reporting the highest talent shortages in five years. Although many companies recognise the impact these shortages will have on their bottom line, more than one in five is struggling to address the issue.

The Chartered Institute of Professional Development (CIPD)/ Hays 2013 Resourcing and Talent Planning survey in the UK shows a threefold increase in the number of employers reporting difficulties in recruiting well-qualified people, from 20% in 2009 to 62% in 2013 (based on the responses of 462 UK-based HR workers). Managerial and professional vacancies are the hardest to fill (52% of responding employers said this) followed by technical specialists (46%), particularly in the manufacturing and production sector.

However, the CIPD/Hays survey revealed that some of the difficulty in recruiting is because skilled workers are reluctant to move jobs during a time of economic uncertainty. It shows that the rate of labour turnover has declined steadily since the start of the financial crisis in 2008. One in six organisations reported that a shortage of skilled job applicants has contributed to recruitment difficulties.

A phoney war?

Employers certainly think they are experiencing talent shortages, but is this really the case? Is the current difficulty in recruiting skilled workers more to do with their reluctance to move jobs than any real decrease in their numbers?

There is an argument that genuine talent shortages would lead to rising wages and lower rates of unemployment for skilled workers such as university graduates. Yet few developed countries are seeing any rise in wages and unemployment rates have risen in many of them.

Mark Price, a labour economist at the US-based Keystone Research Center, points to the number of manufacturers complaining about the shortage of skilled workers in the United States. In 2011, there were reportedly 60,000 vacancies in qualified skilled posts within the US manufacturing sector. "If there's a skill shortage, there have to be rises in wages," Price says. "It's basic economics." Yet the evidence from organisations such as the US Bureau of Labour Statistics is that wages have either stalled or are even falling in the manufacturing sector.

Business leaders, policymakers and economists in the United States have had a vigorous debate about the possibility of a phoney war for talent. A notable figurehead for those who doubt the claims of serious skills shortages is Peter Cappelli, professor of management at the Wharton School, University of Pennsylvania. In his 2012 book *Why Good People Cannot Get Jobs*, he argues that there is no real shortage of skilled workers. He believes that the problem is a result of poor recruitment practices and "picky" employers who make unrealistic demands on workers and offer too low pay. He asserts:

> The skills gap story is their [employers'] diagnosis. It's basically saying there's nobody out there, when in fact, it turns out it's typically the case that employers' requirements are crazy, they're not paying enough or their applicant screening is so rigid that nobody gets through.
>
> Searching forever for somebody – that purple squirrel, as they say in IT, that somebody who is so unique and so unusual, so perfect that you never [find] them – that's not a good idea.

Cappelli points to other practices that help suggest skills shortages. American employers, he argues, are placing too great an emphasis on work experience and are turning away qualified and trained candidates. They are unwilling to provide these candidates with the training or skills that would help alleviate apparent talent shortages. Unrealistic "wish lists" are configured into applicant tracking software, again leading to the rejection of qualified candidates.

He also argues that employers are often leaving positions vacant, parcelling out the work to other employees. This is because most internal accounting systems do not help organisations calculate the true cost of unfilled positions, and there is an impression that there is an economic benefit from not filling jobs.

Research by Randstad, a multinational human resources consulting firm based in the Netherlands, confirms that external recruitment processes are taking longer and that employers are choosier. In the UK, for example, successful candidates for senior roles undergo an average of 3.4 interviews, compared with 2.6 in 2008, and for junior roles an average of 2.4 interviews, compared with 1.6.

Psychometric testing is one major reason for lengthening appointments processes. Randstad's survey finds 29% of UK roles now involve some form of psychometric, technical or aptitude testing, compared with 14% in 2008. Vetting candidates, such as checking references and qualifications, delays the hiring process by 15.2 days on average.

Mark Bull, Randstad's UK chief executive, says that employers have become increasingly selective when it comes to interviewing:

Prospective employees have to jump through many more hiring hoops today than they did before the recession. Employers are often looking for more bang for their buck. A skill set that was satisfactory five years ago might not be now, as employers look towards the long-term potential of new hires. It's not enough to demonstrate you can do the job being advertised – you need to show you can develop in the role and bring something valuable to that organisation in the future.

ManpowerGroup has also noted this trend but nonetheless believes there are real talent shortages. Its 2013 survey suggests that "sluggish demand is actually exacerbating talent shortages". Companies are being more selective about potential hires, seeking an exact match instead of taking the time to develop the skills of less-qualified applicants. Weak demand is effectively clogging up the system. The survey concludes:

> *If demand for their products and services was more robust, [employers] would not have the same luxury of time – hence the apparent head-scratcher of listless jobs growth and greater skills shortages.*

Is it possible to reconcile static wages and large numbers of unemployed people, including university graduates in many European countries, with the complaint from business that they cannot find sufficient numbers of skilled workers? The answer, provided by Hays, a UK recruitment company, and Oxford Economics, a global forecasting and analysis company, is that wage pressure and unemployment rates are not accurate indications of skills shortages. Several factors need to be taken into account to understand the market for skilled labour. Hays and Oxford Economics pooled their data to identify seven "components" that together give a better picture of skill shortages:

- **Labour-market participation.** The degree to which a country's talent pool is fully utilised; for example whether women and older workers have access to jobs.
- **Labour-market flexibility.** The legal and regulatory environment faced by business, especially how easily immigrants can fill talent gaps.
- **Wage pressure overall.** Whether real wages are keeping pace with inflation.
- **Wage pressure in high-skill industries.** The pace at which wages in high-skill industries outpace those in low-skill industries.
- **Wage pressure in high-skill occupations.** Rises in wages for highly skilled workers are a short-term indication of skills shortages.
- **Talent mismatches.** The mismatch between the skills needed by businesses and those available, indicated by the number of long-term unemployed and job vacancies.

■ **Educational flexibility.** Whether the education system can adapt to meet the future needs of organisations for talent, especially in the fields of mathematics and science.

With these seven measurements Hays and Oxford Economics created a "global skills index", which they used to analyse the market for skilled labour in 27 key economies across all five regions of the world during 2012.

The result was a clear picture of skills shortages in 16 of the 27 countries. The study concluded that despite rises in unemployment around the world, particularly in North America and Europe, there is "little evidence that this has led to an easing in skill shortages. Indeed, evidence seems to point to a worsening of the situation". Even though wage pressure is weak in the United States, the UK and Ireland, these countries are experiencing the greatest degree of "talent mismatch", where companies are struggling to recruit the skills they need, despite a large pool of available labour.

The index reveals that skill shortages occur for varied reasons within countries. For example:

■ Germany has the highest overall score for skill shortages and is experiencing wage pressures for high-skill industries and occupations; the engineering, IT, utilities and construction sectors have been particularly hard hit. There is an estimated shortage of 76,400 engineers and 38,000 IT professionals.

■ France is experiencing skill shortages for different reasons. Labour-market inflexibility is stopping firms recruiting foreign talent, and there is a "talent mismatch", where skilled workers are opting for jobs in the financial and commercial sectors instead of sectors such as engineering where there are skill shortages.

■ The UK is experiencing skill shortages in sectors such as energy, banking and finance. It has one of the highest scores for talent mismatches, suggesting there is a serious gap between the skills that employers need and those available in the labour market. However, this is not leading to a rise in wages, as the UK's relative openness to migrant labour is enabling employers to attract staff from overseas (although recent changes in employment laws suggest the country is becoming less welcoming).

■ The United States has the highest overall score for skill shortages. There is a strong demand for skilled people in the oil and gas industries, life sciences and information technology. A big problem is a shortage of experienced and skilled workers but an oversupply of people at entry level. Large numbers of people are either unemployed or underemployed in semi-skilled and part-time jobs because of a lack of skills.

Overall, the index provides evidence of both genuine skill shortages and "talent mismatches". Hays and Oxford Economics conclude:

It is clear from our report that while many graduates are out of work, particularly in Europe, at the same time the world is chronically short of particular skills ... Some of the most important skills for driving growth are in shortage on a global basis ...There is a serious disconnect between higher educational bodies, employers and graduates about the skills now needed in the workplace.

Demand for more advanced skills

Part of the problem for organisations and employees is that new and increased skills are required in the workplace. As economies move from being product-based to being knowledge-based, the number of specialist jobs increases. It is hard for employers and educational providers to anticipate these changes. By 2020, the European Centre for Vocational Training predicts that 81% of all jobs in the EU will require "medium and high level qualifications" because of the continuing shift towards knowledge-intensive activities.

Firms operating in knowledge-intensive industries depend on their most capable staff to help create value through intangible assets such as patents, licences and technical know-how. This is asking a lot. To operate at this level, many people need not just specialist knowledge or technical skills, but also higher cognitive skills to equip them to handle the intricacies of decision-making and change.

The twin forces of globalisation and technology have also led economies across the world to become more entwined, adding to the complexity of many jobs and occupations. Firms are now looking for individuals with a range of abilities that might include specialised skills, broader functional skills, industry expertise and knowledge of specific geographical markets.

Four broad areas of skills will be in greatest demand over the next ten years, according to Oxford Economics and Towers Watson, a global professional services firm. Based on a worldwide survey of 352 human resources managers in the first quarter of 2012 and a modelling exercise involving 46 countries and 21 industry sectors, employers will place a premium on the following:

- **Digital skills.** The fast-growing digital economy is increasing the demand for highly skilled technical workers. Companies are looking for staff with social-media-based skills, especially in "digital expression" and marketing literacy. Digital business skills are rated as crucial, particularly in Asia-Pacific, where e-commerce is expanding rapidly as the result of a "new digital technology war" among firms.

- **Agile thinking.** In a period of sustained uncertainty, where economic, political and market conditions can change suddenly, agile thinking and scenario planning are vital. Those respondents from industries with high levels of regulatory and environmental uncertainty, such as life sciences and energy and mining, highlighted the importance of agile thinking. Respondents said that the ability to prepare for multiple scenarios is especially important. HR managers also put a high premium on innovative thinking, dealing with complexity and managing paradox.

- **Interpersonal and communication skills.** Overall, HR managers predict that co-creativity (collaborating with others) and brainstorming skills will be greatly in demand, as will relationship building and teamwork skills. Oxford Economics points out that this reflects the continued corporate shift from a "command-and-control organisation to a more fluid and collaborative style". As companies move to a "networked" corporate world, relationships with suppliers, outsourcing partners and even customers will become more dispersed and more complex. It will take skill to manage these networks and build consensus and collaboration with network partners.

- **Global operating skills.** The ability to manage diverse employees is seen as the most important global operating skill over the next 5–10 years. In the United States, the top global operating skill was understanding international business. According to Jeff Immelt, chairman and CEO of General Electric, employees need skills in both "glocalisation" (where home-market products and services are tailored to the tastes of overseas customers) and reverse innovation (where staff in emerging markets lead innovation and then the company applies these new ideas to mature markets).

McKinsey's research suggests that this "skill inflation" is occurring in many jobs. There has been a significant increase in the number of jobs involving "interaction work" in developed economies – that is, non-routine jobs involving intensive human interactions, complex decision-making and an understanding of context. In the United States, for instance, some 4.1m new jobs involving interaction work were created between 2001 and 2009, compared with a loss of 2.7m "transaction"-based jobs, where work exchanges are routine, automated and often scripted.

The quantity and quality of graduates

Countries are not producing sufficient numbers of highly educated people to keep pace with the needs of employers and to sustain economic development. This is the case in both emerging markets and developed economies, as an analysis of the global labour force by the McKinsey Global Institute in 2012 shows. The research, covering 70 countries which account for 96% of global GDP, suggests a global shortfall of 38m–40m college-educated workers by 2020.

Although the rate of "tertiary educational attainment" has doubled since 1980, advanced economies (some 25 countries with the highest GDP per head in 2010) will have 16m–18m too few graduates by 2020. Demand is likely to outstrip supply because of the expected expansion of knowledge-intensive sectors in advanced economies.

In the United States, the gap could reach 1.5m graduates by the end of this decade. Even China, which has rapidly expanded tertiary education, is forecast to have a shortfall of 23m graduates by 2020.

There is as much a problem with the quality of graduates as their quantity. Work by the World Economic Forum (WEF) shows a growing problem of employability among graduates in many countries. Employability is defined as the skills graduates need to gain employment and work effectively in a company. These include technical skills, industry-based skills and more generic soft skills such as adaptability, time management and the ability to communicate well.

Employers in a number of countries (including China, Russia, Brazil, Italy, Spain and Turkey) expressed concerns about the level of employability of graduates. In China, for example, although 6.4m students graduated in 2009, 2m were still looking for a job one year later. The Chinese Academy of Social Sciences reported that many of these students lacked the skills required by employers.

Only a small number of graduate schools in India comply with international standards. According to the International Institute for Labour Studies, only 25% of Indian graduates and 20% of Russian graduates are considered employable by multinationals. The WEF says there is an urgent need for governments, educational institutions and employers to collaborate to provide graduates with more relevant education and training. But if graduates are to keep pace with changes in the workplace, employers need to help them keep learning and developing throughout their careers.

Demographic trends

Changing demographics are likely to cause substantial shifts in the size and age of workforces around the world. Employers will need to take account of these shifts when they draw up their plans for "sourcing" talented workers, as well as how they manage their existing pool of talented employees.

The war for talent will intensify, given that the global workforce is predicted to decrease over the next two decades at a time when the demand for advanced skills is expected to increase substantially as a result of globalisation and advances in technology. The WEF warns that "the global economy is approaching a demographic shock of a scale not seen since the Middle Ages". It predicts that by 2020, for every five workers who retire, only four young workers will enter the workforce in the majority of OECD countries.

For the first time ever, the EU's working-age population (aged 20–64) is decreasing from a peak of 308.2m in 2012. The number of workers is likely to drop to 265m by 2060. These demographic shifts, which may be tempered by people working longer, would be even bigger but for an assumed net inflow of over 1m (mostly young) migrants a year.

Ageing populations, especially in North America and Europe, will lead to large numbers of experienced workers retiring, with a corresponding loss of skills and experience. According to the US Census Bureau, 10,000 Americans will retire every day between 2010 and 2030. And according to the European Commission, on average, Germany, France and Italy have the oldest population. Germany's declining birth rate, which now stands at 1.38 children per women, has led to predictions of an economic decline in the next two decades.

An ageing population could offer new possibilities for employers and skilled workers, but it could also create a new set of problems. There could be a new willingness to retain the skills of older workers. In the United States, Germany and Italy, there is active consideration of how skilled older workers can be encouraged and supported to continue working. For example, Germany's Cologne Institute for Economic Research recently urged employers to build more attractive working environments to retain employers aged 55 and over. This might require redesigning roles and taking into account health-care benefits as much as pay.

Conversely, employers might find that retaining older workers blocks the career development of younger employees. There is also the possibility that lower-paid employees (who are likely to be less skilled), rather than their more skilled and better-paid peers, will want to take up any offers of continuing employment. The Pew Research Center, an American think-tank, suggests that six in ten of American workers aged between 50 and 61 may have to postpone retirement because they cannot afford to stop work, but just how their wishes can or will be accommodated by employers remains to be seen.

Employers may still have some way to go before they think about older workers as a valuable source of talent. Research from both sides of the Atlantic suggests that employers are reluctant to recruit unemployed older workers, even qualified and experienced ones. Age discrimination is cited as one likely reason that, in the first quarter of 2012, 40% of older unemployed workers (aged between 50 and 59) in the United States had been out of work for a least one year.

In the UK, a 2013 study by the Age and Employment Network covering 729 unemployed workers explored the reasons why they could not obtain full-time work. It concluded that "age discrimination" is rife among employers. Many of the respondents were highly skilled: 47% were managers or senior officials; 43% had a degree or an equivalent qualification; and 57% had some kind of professional qualification. Despite their experience, 18% of the respondents had been unemployed for 6–12 months, 19% for more than one year and 31% for more than two years.

Insufficient skills did not appear to be a problem; three out of four respondents said they had the right skills for their occupation and industry, with managers and officials being most confident. However, the most significant factor affecting their ability to get work was the attitudes (or prejudices) of employers – 83% said recruiters viewed them as too old, and 72% said they saw them as "too experienced or overqualified".

Working populations are also becoming more ethnically diverse, and this may also require employers to confront assumptions or prejudices that might stop them tapping into this growing pool of talent. In the United States, if current trends continue, the demographic profile of the workforce will change dramatically by the middle of this century, according to new population projections developed by the Pew Research Center. It predicts that the population will rise from 296m in 2005 to 438m in 2050, and that new immigrants and their descendants will account for 82% of the growth. Of the 117m people added to the population through new immigration, 67m will be the immigrants themselves, 47m will be their children and 3m will be their grandchildren.

Talent management to the rescue?

There seems no doubt that highly capable employees are in short supply and that employers must make strenuous efforts to find them, keep developing their abilities and make sure that they are not poached by rival firms. Are talent management strategies up to the challenge?

Research for this book reveals that there is an established approach to making the most of gifted employees, but it is beginning to look outmoded and ineffective in the face of the global fight for talent. There is evidence that senior managers and HR managers are highly dissatisfied with their talent programmes, and are looking for new ways to make sure that high-flying employees are identified and nurtured.

During the past decade a model of good practice has been developed which most organisations with a reputation and track record of success in this field try to follow. This model encompasses:

- **Links to graduate entry schemes.** For decades before the term was commonly used, talent management strategies have been closely linked to graduate entry schemes with selection processes (often assessment centres, psychological tests, etc) designed to spot potential talent.

- **Early identification of potential and performance.** Even if this does not occur at graduate entry levels, early identification of both potential and performance form part of most talent management strategies. A popular and commonly used tool to achieve this is the "nine-box grid" (see Figure 1.1), often used in a group setting, which provides multiple perspectives of employees' skills and potential.

- **Targeted and tailored support, development and career planning.** Once "talented" individuals have been identified, they receive targeted and tailored support development and career planning. This may include study opportunities on sponsored MBA or other postgraduate programmes, senior management development programmes (delivered either internally or at prestigious business schools) and systematic cross-disciplinary and cross-geography job rotation to make sure that individuals have management experience in key functions connected to the business strategy. In recent years, particularly in the case of women and ethnic minorities, personalised career management has been supported by coaching, mentoring and the use of "sponsors" (senior managers who champion an individual for promotion).

- **Long-term succession planning linked to talent "pipelines".** Roles filled through this talent "pool" are planned sometimes decades in advance through a complex system of succession planning and talent "pipelines". The progress of individuals towards their allotted roles is reviewed regularly (often on a quarterly or twice-yearly basis) by talent review committees made up of a combination of specialist HR managers, line managers and members of the senior management team. Often the organisation's chief executive or other board members chair these committees. This ensures that the roles under scrutiny are linked closely to the requirements of the business strategy and the wishes of stakeholders and shareholders (institutional shareholders are now looking closely at organisations' succession-planning processes when making investment decisions).

- **Exposure to senior management.** Often with the backing of the chief executive, prospective candidates for senior roles in the talent pipeline are systematically exposed to the organisation's existing senior management through formal and informal briefings, workshops and discussion groups. Ensuring that this occurs has become an important role for the chief executive (see Indra Nooyi's comments in Chapter 2).

A 2011 CIPD report provides a snapshot of talent management approaches in UK-based businesses:

- Talent management activities are most commonly focused on two groups – high-potential employees (77% of responding firms said this) and senior managers (64% of responding firms).

- Small and medium-sized firms (SMEs) use talent management more than do larger organisations (more than 250 employees) both to attract key staff (41% of SMEs compared with 20% of larger firms) and to retain them (50% of SMEs compared with 35% of larger firms).

- Some 77% of very large firms (more than 5,000 employees) have talent management programmes, and some 66% of them focus their efforts on senior managers.

Talent is a relative concept

By and large, companies formulate their own definitions of talent and potential. It is safe to say that talented people are highly intelligent and gifted, with a particular blend of skills, knowledge and personal attributes. However, most organisations define talent in the context of their business or industry. Individuals are given the label of talented because they have attributes that are of great value to the business and hard to develop or replicate in others.

The firms featured in the case studies in this book have their own definitions of talent, but the common focus is on individuals who either make, or have the potential to make, a disproportionately strong impact on their part of the business. In other words, their knowledge and skill make such a difference that their organisations can ill-afford to lose them.

In some of the case studies, a star employee is someone with rare specialist skills. These skills are in great demand in the labour market and rival companies may be trying to poach these individuals. However, the majority of the case studies focus on leadership ability, and the firms featured arrived at a definition of talent by identifying key roles in the organisation that needed to be filled by the most capable individuals in the immediate or medium-term future (that is, succession planning).

Organisations have different talent requirements, which mirror the size and complexity of the business. These definitions or "talent profiles" effectively segment talent and form the basis of different talent pools. These could include, for example:

■ technical specialists, especially in areas key to the organisation's core capabilities;

■ individuals with hard-to-recruit skills;

■ bright individuals from underrepresented groups whom the organisation wishes to advance into more senior positions;

■ the best-performing graduates or school leavers;

■ managers with the potential to move into senior management positions at the local, national or international level.

Regardless of the mix of specialist and management/leadership skills, talent is usually defined in terms of exceptional performance or high potential. The weighting of these two attributes is decided by senior managers in line with the organisation's immediate and long-term priorities. There is often an implicit judgment about selecting individuals whose behaviour and values fit with those of the organisation.

How performance and potential are measured is for senior managers to decide. In many cases, the definition of exceptional performance is laid out in competency frameworks and appraisal systems. Defining high potential can be more difficult and might include a range of assessment tools such as development centres, psychometric testing and, inevitably, the personal judgment of those whose insights into talent are widely respected.

Organisations often use a nine-box grid to map individuals in terms of potential and performance (see Figure 1.1). Existing performance-management processes will be relied upon to keep monitoring and improving the performance of weak or solid performers. Technical specialists are often grouped in the bottom right box and the organisation, while valuing them highly, may not feel they need any extra opportunities to fulfil their potential. A talent management programme will generally focus on individuals in the top right box.

Some organisations opt for the simple solution of automatically placing a percentage of its top performers, identified through existing appraisal processes, into a talent pool. At Network Rail, for example, the talent pool was created for individuals who had reached the two uppermost bands for senior managers. However, the company has

FIG 1.1 **Nine-box grid of performance and potential**

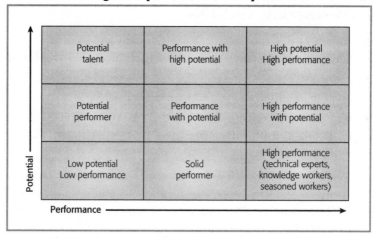

other selection criteria. Managers must be capable of moving up an additional band (into the highest senior management band or the director-level band) and be capable of moving across Network Rail as well as upwards. Approximately 100 managers constitute the talent pool at any one time.

Other organisations favour informal approaches to defining talent and identifying high-flyers. In an international manufacturing company, there is an informal network of senior HR managers who keep an eye on promising employees. Known as "TalentWatch", the network both identifies talented individuals and promotes their advancement by ensuring they are allocated to temporary "special projects", which will stretch them and enhance their personal reputation.

Well-established – but not well done

After a decade of experimentation, many companies still struggle with their talent strategies and are by no means confident that their approaches will guarantee enough leaders and specialists of the right calibre for their current and future needs.

A global survey by the Boston Consultancy Group (BCG) in 2010 suggests that many companies do not have a clear strategy for finding and keeping the best people. Covering 5,561 business leaders from 109 countries, the survey revealed that:

- some 60% of respondents said they lacked a well-defined strategy to source talent or to address their succession challenges;
- more than 33% ranked their company as having no strategy at all, and only 2% cited a strong, comprehensive strategy;
- on average, respondents said their chief executives and other senior managers spent less than nine days a year on activities related to talent management;
- talent management activities were narrowly focused, mainly on high-potential employees, with promising junior employees receiving least attention;
- only 1% of respondents said talent plans were aligned with the company's business-planning cycle.

BCG concluded that too many companies are "relying on serendipity to meet their current and future talent needs, incurring unnecessary business risk".

Even human resources managers doubt their own track record in talent management. A 2012 McKinsey study describes HR staff as nearly "paralysed" by the scale of challenges facing them, with many feeling they are failing to keep pace with an unpredictable business environment. They identified talent management as a particularly daunting area. Only 32% had "high confidence" in their talent strategy or actions.

Emily Lawson, head of McKinsey's global human capital practice, says the uncertainties of the current business environment are making it genuinely difficult for firms to assess the effectiveness of their strategies. She comments:

> I can count on the fingers of two hands the robust talent strategies that I have actually seen – where the numbers have been done robustly and are modelled three to five years out where it is clearly understood what it is going to take to compete in a particular market. I think it is very hard.

Talent strategies take a long time to play out. There is still a misalignment between what goes on inside companies and what would strategically benefit them in terms of talent. Also in the wake of the 2008 downturn, companies stopped undertaking a lot of the discretionary activities in areas like career planning and mentoring that play such an important part in the process.

Can talent still be "managed"?

For all this focused investment of time, effort and financial resources, the question remains: can the current model of talent management help companies compete in an intensely competitive and global market for talent?

The research for this book suggests that there are a number of assumptions underpinning the current model that may no longer be relevant, including:

- management and leadership potential can be spotted early;
- this definition of potential will still be relevant in five or even ten years' time;
- getting to the top young is good for the organisation;
- if you get senior management right, it will help the business;
- career moves can be planned and achieved;
- the concept of systematic development is sound and should be managed by the company;
- the individuals under the spotlight are willing pawns in the game.

The last point is the most important one.

Spotting potential

Taking hard and fast judgments about potential is difficult enough in stable times, but in an unpredictable environment they become risky. As outlined above, the fast pace of change in some industries is making it difficult for firms to anticipate the skills they will need to compete successfully. This is a blind spot for many firms, often because the definition of what constitutes talent is heavily influenced by the existing senior management team. This increases the danger of firms producing an over-homogeneous pool of successors at a time when many experts and simple common sense stress the need for diversity – a theme that is explored in more depth in Chapter 4.

Chris Benko, vice-president of global talent management at Merck, an American pharmaceutical company, comments:

> *Transforming the company and the way we think about talent is very challenging ... Most of the formative experiences of our senior leaders were in the late 1990s and the early part of this century – which was a heyday for the pharmaceutical industry.*
>
> *Now we need to move leaders pass their comfort zones to think about what it is going to take to develop in a way that is contrary to what led to their success and the success of our company.*

Some organisations have no time for high-potential development schemes. Liane Hornsey, vice-president of people operations at Google, a multinational corporation specialising in internet-related services and products, says that she "detests" such schemes. Google, by contrast, offers all its employees the opportunity to put themselves forward for promotion based on their track record and performance:

> *We never hire because we have to get a task done. Every single hire that we make, be that in the most junior of roles, be that in the most junior customer service position for example, we will hire someone who we think has the potential to be a very senior leader.*

In firms that adopt this approach, a strong culture that motivates bright employees to put themselves forward for advancement and development plays a far more important role than the detailed systems and processes for talent selection and development. Responsibility for career management and development is shared more effectively between the individual and the organisation. Getting the culture right is crucial, as Hornsey stresses:

> *Over I don't know how many years, I have learned one thing. And that one thing is that if you don't have a fertile soil in which you plant seeds, it doesn't matter how intellectually robust and how brilliant your processes and your programmes are, they will fail. But if you have a robust soil, and a brilliant culture, the processes and*

the programmes can be pretty weak but they will work – because having the right culture is absolutely the bedrock to making sure you develop talent.

Talent-based culture is covered in more detail in Chapter 5.

Keeping pace with business needs

Traditional talent management has generally focused on an integrated set of activities to make sure that there is a reliable supply of seasoned managers who will form the next generation of senior managers and leaders. Much of the focus of HR staff has been on activities and programmes which, although important, have arguably taken on a life of their own. This is covered in more detail in Chapter 3.

Becky Snow, global talent director at Mars, points out that talent management schemes are like huge tankers that are slow to manoeuvre if the organisation decides (or is forced) to move in different directions at short notice – an increasing likelihood in an uncertain and volatile world (see Chapter 3). Steering this tanker has prevented talent heads from playing a sufficiently strategic role in the business. If companies are to compete for talent effectively, they need to pay much more attention to achieving a tighter alignment between the needs of a business and the product of its talent management strategies. This is explored in more depth in Chapter 2.

Too much focus on the top

Most talent strategies focus heavily on getting a small number of people to the top of the organisation – often at the expense of everyone else. Yet there is less and less of a guarantee that the genuinely talented people the company seeks for its senior roles are willing or eager to invest their lives and their careers in reaching this goal.

Conventional talent management schemes rarely accommodate:

- mavericks and outsiders who are creative and innovative in their thinking but do not perform well using traditional appraisal measures;
- those with entrepreneurial aspirations who are frustrated by the lack of opportunity to engage in business start-up activities

or (more cynically) use a corporate career as a stepping stone to launch their own enterprise (in both cases the organisation loses precious skills that it badly needs);

■ late starters or those recruited later in their careers who are normally too old to be on the high-flyer track even though they might vary the pool of talent at the organisation's disposal;

■ those in peripheral careers within the company (technology, research, data processing) or those who want to make sideways moves for personal reasons or because they prefer the line of work;

■ those who are not sufficiently motivated by the prize on offer to pay the price they have to pay to climb the corporate ladder.

Chapters 4 and 6 explore how talent strategies need to be broadened to appeal to the needs and wants of these largely untapped groups of employees.

Conclusion: willing pawns?

Traditional talent management assumes that high-flying employees want to get to the top of the pile and will do whatever their firms require to get there. However, a new generation of talented workers may not be willing or motivated to stay with one employer for long, whatever the financial rewards and career opportunities on offer.

This makes long-term career planning much more difficult for organisations. Chapter 6 looks at how firms can retain the skills and creativity of former workers through associate and consultancy positions or by creating internal structures that enable intrapreneurs – those with entrepreneurial skills and aspirations who are willing to work inside organisations – to engage in business start-up activity and ideas incubators. These new relationships and work arrangements will help organisations anticipate and respond quickly to changes in the marketplace.

The following chapters look at how firms are changing their talent strategies in a volatile business environment where gifted employees have the ability to pursue opportunities virtually anywhere in the world.

2 Devising and implementing a talent strategy

Our talent management plan is designed annually by business heads and our HR people. But it is the business heads that drive the talent agenda and keep it alive and customised to each business unit. They hold a quarterly review to assess the progress of the plan and whether it is furthering their strategic goals.

Joydeep Bose, president and global head of human resources,
Olam International

IN MATURE AND EMERGING MARKETS alike, the ability to implement strategy depends on having staff with the right experience and knowledge positioned in the right places across the business at the right time.

Having the right people in place for the current and emerging needs of a business is not easy. First, the talent implications of the organisation's strategy must be understood – and the more thought-provoking and clear the strategy is the easier this will be. Second, there must be effective processes for making sure that enough high-calibre staff are recruited or brought up through the ranks and given appropriate training and experience.

As the previous chapter outlined, many firms are struggling to recruit enough talented people, either because of skills shortages, mismatches between the location of jobs and suitably qualified people, or because of the difficulty of gaining access to hitherto untapped groups of talented workers. It has also become harder for firms to make longer-term predictions about the skills they will need and where these should be deployed across the business.

Staying ahead or playing catch-up?

Research for this book suggests that even firms that have a talent strategy lack confidence in it. Unilever, a multinational consumer-goods company, for one, has doubts about the effectiveness of its talent plans. It developed a new ten-year strategic plan in 2011 in response to the shift of economic power eastwards, the increasing focus on environmental sustainability and other trends. The company aims to double its turnover from €44 billion in 2010 to €80 billion by 2020.

Doug Baillie, president of western Europe and a member of the executive committee, admits that he is daunted by the talent implications of the new strategy, especially the goal of doubling the value of the business, commenting:

> This is bold; it is really ambitious. We haven't managed to grow turnover by 7% a year in our history for ten consecutive years.
>
> The big question about integrating talent into strategy is whether we lay the road ahead of the business or follow behind. We have big goals. How do we go about it? How do I take that ambition and that strategy? How do we put talent right into the middle of that and try to drive it?

As well as needing more skilled leaders and managers, Unilever wants them to come from a wider assortment of nationalities. Almost all the projected growth will come from developing and emerging markets. Some 60% of Unilever's business today is in these markets, but by 2020 the company estimates that this will be anywhere between 70% and 80%. Baillie explains:

> If you think that 60–80% of our business will be in the South and the East of the world, the challenge is where do we find the leaders to lead this business? Our top 100 leaders consist of 22 different nationalities. This sounds not too bad but of those 100 leaders, 60% are British, Dutch or Indian. We have to develop more leaders from other geographies.

HR and business heads now work closely together to formulate a talent plan that will support the new strategy. In simple terms, the talent plan has three components:

- **Talent gaps** across the business. HR works with business heads once a year to identify which leadership, management and functional skills are needed, how these align with roles and responsibilities, and whether the talent processes are producing people who will be able to plug these skill gaps.
- **Talent supply.** Most of the focus is on management trainees and a smaller proportion of people who are recruited mid-career.
- **Talent development.** Unilever prefers to recruit high-potential individuals at the start of their careers and take them through a structured development programme.

Unilever tries to keep talent plans aligned with the business strategy by incorporating the annual talent plans within business units into a three-year strategic review for the whole organisation. In addition, the top management team takes responsibility for the development of the top 100 managers worldwide, including senior vice-presidents, vice-presidents and directors. Baillie comments:

We spend a lot of time on the top 100 leaders. We regularly talk about them at our executive meetings. We spend a whole day every year putting them into a fairly standard nine-box performance grid and ranking them. We talk a lot about getting the right people for the right job and making sure that we have identified where we want them to be in five years' time. We also ensure these individuals have opportunities to meet the executive team.

Despite joint planning between HR and business heads, a talent plan that directly feeds into strategy planning cycles and the close involvement of the top management team, Baillie still wonders if his talent plan will fuel Unilever's growth or act as a brake:

The question that keeps me most awake at night is do I have the talent to achieve our goals? Can I get the talent in quickly enough to get ahead of the growth – or am I going to play catch-up over the next couple of years?

It appears that few other companies are taking the matter so seriously, however. A 2010 study of FTSE 100 companies by Heidrick

& Struggles, a global executive search firm, found that while some senior managers believed having the right people on board and managing the process of recruiting, developing and getting the best out of them could be a source of competitive advantage, many companies do little more than engage in filling vacancies.

Furthermore, although Baillie is a member of Unilever's senior management team, has been employed by Unilever for decades and has a previous track record running geographical regions inside the company, the Heidrick & Struggles report found this kind of career profile an exception for those in charge of talent strategies. In the FTSE 100 study, only 17% of those surveyed reported directly to the CEO. Some 90% had spent their whole career in HR. When asked "How well do you think your organisation manages talent?", they gave an average score of 6 out of 10. Significantly, the average length of time the role of head of talent had existed in the company was only five years and the average time those surveyed had been in the role was three years.

David Smith, managing director of the talent and organisation performance service at Accenture, a multinational management consulting company, confirms the patchy nature of corporate commitment revealed by the survey:

> A great many of our clients are putting talent management at the heart of their business strategy and are integrating it into their thinking and decision-making and driving it very strategically. The key point is the integration into business strategy. Talent management is front and centre in their scenario planning and analytics.
>
> At the other end of the spectrum there are some organisations that pay only lip service to talent management. They talk about the importance of it yet when you work with business executives, it is apparent that it is not rated very highly. There is a focus on day-to-day HR administration but not really talent management.
>
> In the middle there are those who say it is hard to get the right sponsorship from the top and to get senior executives to carve out specific time to deal with recruitment and retention and leadership development issues.

Much of the problem is the difficulty of getting the HR function to operate at a strategic level. McKinsey's 2012 analysis in "The State of Human Capital" of the ills besetting the HR function showed that many HR staff felt they did not have the necessary status or capability to work effectively with operational heads or the top management team. Responses from the business units of 72 firms confirmed this, giving the lowest ranking to how well the HR function "sourced" and recruited talented staff. Overall, the business units ranked HR functions as more effective at transactional tasks such as payroll administration than at strategic tasks which added value to the business.

Devising a talent strategy

Organisations must devise talent plans that reflect their strategic priorities. The research for this book suggests that the formulation of a plan that has the best chance of being effective involves carrying out strategic and talent reviews and setting up systems for measurement and evaluation, accountability and governance.

Strategic review

The top management team, heads of operations and the talent management team work together to build a shared understanding of the strategic goals for the whole business as well as the priorities for each business unit. This review should

- incorporate discussions about the cultural values and behaviours that the company desires and how these help employees to achieve or aspire to outstanding performance;

- give the talent management function specific information about the yearly business plan and also the strategic direction for the next 3-5 years.

With these priorities clear, senior leaders can identify the capabilities that help achieve the company's strategic objectives and provide a competitive edge. These capabilities are identified initially at a high level to make sure that they directly underpin the strategic plan and are not just tactical or operational skills, which, although important, do not have as much of an impact on business performance and profits. Operational heads and the talent management team then break down each capability into its constituent parts, such as specific skills, knowledge and expertise. They look at how these skill sets enable each business unit to deliver their part of the strategic plan.

This analysis should reveal the roles where knowledge and expertise are deployed for maximum business value. These are not automatically senior leadership or management roles. They also extend to technical and specialist roles or to previously overlooked roles – for example, positions within the organisation that help make sure that vital expertise from one part of the business flows to another. Part of this review may necessitate a fresh look at knowledge-management processes across the business.

The HR team should also review its own ways of working and thinking to make sure that its processes for recruitment, selection, learning and development, appraisal, reward and recognition, and so on foster the skills, cultural values and behaviours most critical to business performance.

Talent review

The aim of a talent review is to assess how well employees are performing currently in the critical roles, identified by the strategic review, and their potential to move into more demanding roles. Some of the required data will be held centrally by HR, but, almost certainly, the team carrying out the review will need to speak directly to operational and line managers to get feedback about the performance and potential of key individuals.

Managers often struggle to make judgments about potential, and if this is the case, part of the strategic review should include a discussion of it to make sure that the organisation is not working to historical and possibly outdated notions of potential. The top management team is just as likely to be as prone as anyone else to unconscious bias on what potential is and how you spot it. Managers have to leave aside the factors that made them successful in their careers and think objectively about what an outstanding leader, manager or specialist will look like in five years or so. Devising or revising a nine-box grid of performance and potential related to future business plans is helpful in getting to a shared definition (see Figure 1.1).

The review should also look at the talent work that is currently taking place, such as high-potential and leadership development programmes, or diversity initiatives designed to accelerate the development of promising individuals from an underrepresented group of employees. One important question is whether there are any activities that are not badged as talent management but support its agenda, such as staff exchanges, going on between the organisation and a valued supplier or strategic partner.

As part of the review, gap analysis will help identify gaps in skills necessary to carry out the business's strategy and plans, and whether any critical roles are unfilled. Succession planning is a crucial factor here as it may well be that insufficient numbers of potential successors have been identified for certain critical roles.

A gap analysis is a standard part of workforce planning that looks at current operational needs in the context of short-term plans. A talent-based gap analysis takes a more strategic line in that it:

- focuses on hiring and/or training needs as part of a talent strategy;
- is integrated with the company's strategic planning process;
- draws on a wide source of data, both internally and externally, such as industry benchmarks;
- looks at strategic needs both current and future, and makes judgments about operational needs based on this wider context.

This analysis determines whether the right talented people are in the right place at the right time. Looking at the intersections between these three factors can highlight where talent planning needs to be improved. For example:

- **Right people, wrong time.** For example, people who might not be being used currently because of a downturn in markets but who the organisation does not want to lose as it takes too much time and money to replace them when demand increases. The organisation must therefore determine its strategy for retaining and motivating them.

■ **Wrong people.** The people in place are not the right people to perform the work. This suggests a misalignment between HR processes and the business strategy. Learning and development processes may not be keeping pace with changing business needs. There may be some flaws in appraisal and promotion decisions that are leading to a mismatch between roles and people.

■ **Right people, wrong place.** For example, people who can do the work but are in the wrong location as a result of a reorganisation and constraints on mobility. The organisation therefore needs to reduce barriers to staff mobility, make more creative use of temporary assignments and virtual working, or relocate work to where it can be done by the most skilful employees.

Once the talent review has identified any shortages of talent, an organisation has three options:

■ **Buy talent** through external recruitment.

■ **Build talent** through tailored learning and development programmes that involve work experiences that will help pinpoint as well as nurture talent.

■ **Borrow talent** by resorting to temporary workers or outsourcing.

These three options are discussed later in this chapter. A fourth option that is rarely pursued by firms but is likely to become more important is broadening talent. This entails building an "ecosystem" of talent by extending talent processes to incorporate previously overlooked groups of individuals within and outside the business; this is the focus of Chapter 6.

Measurement and evaluation, accountability and governance

The talent plan that emerges from the strategic and talent reviews should have the following components:

- a clear strategic vision and set of objectives that are explicitly linked to the overall business strategy;
- a set of critical success factors and measures for evaluating progress and return on investment;
- the scope of talent management in terms of which groups of employees have been targeted and the main talent activities;
- detailed costs;
- risks and dependencies – the internal and external factors that will influence the success of the talent plan;
- the governance structure to ensure that problems are managed and resolved and everyone is held accountable to the plan, including the talent management function and any operational heads or line managers who are involved in implementing the plan;
- an internal communications strategy to ensure that everyone understands the aims of the talent plan and why it is important to the business. A compelling business case is especially important if some parts of the business do not see the need for any form of extra support for high-flying employees.

It is only through some system of measurement and evaluation that the effectiveness (and credibility) of the talent management strategy can be gauged. There are a number of measures that can be used, including:

- overall costs (development programmes, cost of time spent overall on talent management, internal resources such as a dedicated talent management office);
- turnover and retention levels in critical roles;
- length of time required to fill vacancies;
- the percentages of key roles that are filled internally and externally;
- employee engagement data;
- average performance ratings for new employees in critical roles;

- promotions from within the various talent pools within a specified timeframe;
- savings from recruitment costs;
- increases in the number of successors in succession plans for critical roles;
- survey results gauging the effectiveness of development programmes. This could be based on how the participants rated the experience as well as workplace feedback to assess whether their performance improved.

Jan Hill, a partner at Orion Partners, a consulting firm, says talent management will gain more credibility if measurements are explicitly linked to business results. She explains:

> Most organisations measure the health of their talent processes; for example, looking at the number of high-potential employees ... HR then struggles to demonstrate the value of its activities.
> While these measures are important, relying on them works only if senior stakeholders make the connection between the talent process and achieving business goals.

Foundations of a talent strategy: buy, borrow, build

As outlined earlier, companies have three options when it comes to filling talent gaps: to buy, borrow or build.

Buying talent

An obvious choice when a company needs particular skills or expertise that it does not have the time or ability to develop in existing staff is to buy in that talent. The task is then to source this expertise, and offer the right set of inducements to recruit and retain individuals with the desired skills.

The downside is that buying talent can be costly as the going rate for sought-after specialists is high and they are often in a strong negotiating position. Swift recruitment processes and flexible remuneration packages help in getting such people on board, but just as important will be that the work is satisfyingly stretching and that it enables someone to remain at – or reach – the forefront of their field. Boredom and repetition are likely to send them into the arms of rival firms.

The competition to recruit the top performers in an occupation or industry is most likely to be won by firms that excel in employer "branding", where they position themselves as an employer "of choice" or a "must have" name on an individual's job résumé. Firms will pay a lot for IT specialists and a prolific amount of money is spent on buying in talent in the financial sector. But acquiring talent can be the only option for firms that are growing rapidly or where there is intense competition for certain skills so as to capitalise on a new business opportunity, such as business analytics or social-media-based marketing.

Borrowing talent

When there is a temporary need for specialist skills it makes sense to borrow or "rent" what is required by contracting with, for example, freelancers, independent consultants, staff on secondment or firms that will supply staff.

This form of flexible labour has always been important to firms, but in uncertain times such flexibility becomes more attractive. It enables firms to assemble new combinations of skills in swift response to sudden shifts in their environment. It provides firms with access to a wider pool of talent, especially in the case of work that can be performed in any location. And although freelance specialists may charge top-dollar rates, it can make good economic sense – providing temporary workers do not in effect become expensively permanent.

Temporary workers, who are able to carry out their work remotely, can be hired through traditional recruitment processes or through online marketplaces, known as "talent exchanges". Employers specify what they want done remotely or "virtually", and interested individuals then bid for the assignment. These talent exchanges, sometimes described as "cloud talent sourcing", enable firms to access a global pool of talent.

According to *The Economist*, online marketplaces like ODesk and Elance have grown rapidly. The value of work contracted online exceeded $1 billion in 2012 and is forecast to double to $2 billion by 2014 and to reach $5 billion by 2018. ODesk brokered 35m hours of work in 2012 (over 50% more than in 2011), divided among 1.5m tasks, at a total cost of $360m to its corporate customers. The value of work on Elance rose by 40% in 2012 to more than $200m. Some 69% of Elance's freelancers have a university degree or equivalent professional qualification and their work assignments often last several months.

According to the Human Capital Institute, the type of work done by temporary workers is changing. The increase of specialised work and the heavy reliance on project work in knowledge-based organisations mean that it now involves those with expertise in such fields as engineering, IT, health care, accounting and finance. In a 2010 survey conducted by Accenture and the International Association of Outsourcing Professionals, just over 40% of respondents indicated that outsourcing at their organisations was increasingly focused on knowledge-based activities.

The role of HR is to act as a "talent broker", helping achieve a tight fit between a skilled individual employed on a temporary basis and specific tasks and projects across a business. The more a business relies on such temporary talent, the more it needs to consider how to manage such people and whether they should be included in talent management processes, such as learning and development initiatives. This topic is explored in greater depth in Chapter 6.

Building talent

A larger firm will seek to build its own talent by creating a reliable "pipeline" of high-potential and high-performing employees. The aim is to spot rising stars early and to invest in their careers in the expectation that they will progress to senior positions in the business.

Typically, these individuals are placed in a talent pool where their progress is monitored and where they are given extra opportunities for training and development. To keep talented people moving through the pipeline there is an emphasis on performance management, so any weaknesses or developmental needs can be spotted early on. If they live up to expectations, these high-flyers are slotted into succession plans as they rise up the organisation and gain greater experience.

The notion of keeping talent moving around the business is critical. HR and line managers often work together to make sure that promising employees gain experience in different functions and business units. This requires career mapping, where the organisation (probably HR) devises a "road-map" for employees outlining the skills, experiences and qualifications they need to move from one job to another, and longer-term development plans, which might include a combination of coaching, on-the-job learning, management development programmes and further study towards professional qualifications.

This approach is most commonly taken by larger businesses, especially multinationals like Unilever, Mars and Olam International (see below) because they have the resources to provide promising employees with targeted training and development and a wide range of work experiences, especially international assignments.

The biggest challenge is to make sure that every part of an organisation is clear about what it means by talent so that high-flyers are identified, nurtured and developed equally well across the organisation. HR processes need to reflect these definitions (so using a company-wide competency framework helps ensure consistency in decisions about performance, promotion and development, and so on). Fragmented processes can also lead to some individuals getting lost in the system or being held back by a boss who may not want to lose them or who feels sufficiently threatened by them to block their progress.

Performance data on talented staff must be collated so that there is strong evidence for decisions affecting them. And other data should be gathered from across the organisation to demonstrate the link between investing in promising staff and their impact on the business. However, as Chapter 3 argues, this intensive process-based approach can lead to an unwieldy talent "machine" which causes HR staff to spend too much time in transactional activities instead of taking a more strategic role.

The options of buying, borrowing or building talent are not mutually exclusive. Indeed, over time the majority of organisations will do all three to meet different needs in different circumstances.

Olam International

Olam International is a global integrated supply chain manager and processor of agricultural products and food ingredients. Its talent management strategy is set against the background of the decision taken in 2009 to expand its activities. As well as trading commodities like cotton, palm, rubber, coffee, rice and edible nuts, Olam decided to farm, source, manufacture, package, market and distribute these commodities – what the firm calls going upstream and downstream in the supply chain.

The company embarked on a spending spree (which came to an end in spring 2013 after savage criticism by a prominent American hedge fund, which engaged in some large-scale short-selling of the company's stock), acquiring 30 agricultural assets such as almond orchards, dairy farms, rubber plantations and processing plants and in the process boosting its workforce by 30%.

The pace and extent of the growth presented a number of HR priorities.

Embed a common culture

The first was embedding a common culture into a disparate set of newly acquired processing facilities and plantations so that all technical specialists and managers signed up to and were motivated by the company's shared values of entrepreneurship, ownership, integrity, mutual respect, stretch and ambition. Janaky Grant, head of learning and development at Olam, explains:

> We have a group of business leaders who form the Culture and Values Standing Committee. When Olam re-looked at its business strategy in 2008–09, the committee played a key role in questioning our existing core values and whether they were going to hold up in a larger and more diversified business.
>
> The result was that we redefined our core values so that they could be applied across the organisation including the newly acquired entities. We organised forums to communicate the shared values.
>
> We also held sessions where people discussed the dilemmas of behaving according to these values in practice. Our people are often spread out working in remote plantations, farms and manufacturing plants so it was useful to debate various dilemmas and achieve a shared understanding of the desired values..

Identify and develop new skills

The second was identifying and developing the new skills the company was going to need. Joydeep Bose, president and global head of human resources at Olam, stresses:

> In the past, the role of a manager was managing an enterprise. Leaders were managing large teams, distribution networks and logistics. Now, the organisation has invested in manufacturing assets, investment projects and plantations. The new group of managers who run these businesses require deep expertise in these different parts of the supply chain.

The company focused on drawing up what it terms "domain-specific competencies" – the skills that apply to each part of the business such as sourcing products (requiring, for example, skill in procurement); trading (trading insights, hedging derivatives); packaging and distribution; and marketing products. To help build these capabilities, the company established "communities of practice" to connect plant managers, production and quality managers across businesses based in various African and Asian countries. These committees meet regularly to build a shared knowledge base. "They talk about challenges and share their success stories," says Grant.

Identify and build global leaders internally

The third was to set in place an accelerated process of identifying and building global leaders internally who could manage capital-intensive businesses and assets and pursue new business opportunities that were emerging as Olam pursued its growth strategy.

Each year on average 30% of the total people hired are recruited through a graduate trainee programme. This is globally co-ordinated across universities and business schools in Asia, Africa, Australia and North and South America. Graduate trainees are typically placed in commercial and operational roles, but they go through 18 months of training before starting to ensure they have a rounded understanding of the company's businesses, operating processes, culture and values and the various roles across the global organisation.

The graduate trainee programme is linked to a global assignment talent pool (GATP), which consists of 750 managers in critical positions across the 65 countries in which Olam operates. Bose explains:

People are selected to the pool based on roles in the organisation that we consider as having a higher impact – and people who demonstrate a strategic fit in the organisation and its desired values and behaviours. These roles have a global dimension. These individuals need to acquire a wider perspective beyond the boundaries of their countries.

These people will be moved across Olam's many products, geographies and functional boundaries. However, we want our general managers to acquire more specialised knowledge, so we expect them to be in each position for at least four to five years before they take on another role.

Olam has also headhunted more experienced staff to fill newly created specialist global functions that provide across-the-board support for the various businesses.

Succession to specific roles is reviewed regularly by a committee comprising business heads and HR managers. Any talent management expenditure is discussed by the committee and assessed on the basis of whether it is aligned to the business's needs. Olam's goal is that HR practices are led and managed by the business heads themselves.

For example, Steve Driver, head of manufacturing and technical services, a global function that was created from scratch in 2011, sets standards and procedures to ensure consistency across manufacturing. He also works with HR to provide training and development for high-level skills that help manufacturing teams implement growth plans (such as buying a new manufacturing plant), achieve efficiencies and build capability in manufacturing processes.

Driver is responsible for talent processes for the country managers, heads of business units and plant managers who oversee or run manufacturing facilities. He and his leadership team work with the central HR team as a "strategic partner", as he explains:

We work extremely well together. We meet three times a year to ensure we have the required skills and capabilities within manufacturing. We agree our direction, based on a balanced scorecard analysis of the function. A lot of our work has been around defining model profiles for various roles. We spend a lot of time running workshops in different regions explaining this approach.

Driver believes it is his (not HR's) responsibility to get buy-in from business heads to sign up to the new capabilities required by the new strategy. He asserts:

> *Putting in place these processes, structures and disciplines is one thing. The second thing is getting management support. This is how I spend the bulk of my time – explaining to the regional heads why we are doing things differently and getting their buy-in.*
>
> *These are aggressive alpha-male MBAs who have been driving the business very successfully. It was a question of sitting down with them and telling them – and telling them again – that the last thing anyone wants to do is to stifle growth or entrepreneurialism, but there are certain things that have to be done differently. I emphasise that this is value-creating. These are smart guys. It might not be their natural inclination – but they get it.*

With the new standards and competencies in place, the manufacturing and technical services leadership team has recently conducted a talent review for top managers across the globe, based on performance data from the annual appraisal process. This review looks at their strengths and weaknesses as well as judgments about their potential, with the aim of designing longer-term career paths.

Driver emphasises the importance of a "can do" approach to talent management when an organisation is expanding as rapidly as Olam:

> *In such a dynamic business, it is hard to stay ahead of the curve. You have to be nimble. A gap appears and you plug it.*
>
> *We don't have lots of meetings about talent management. We sit down with the HR team, we set out our business priorities and our talent agenda. We don't make a big deal of it and we don't analyse it to death, we just get on with it.*

Gaining sponsorship from the business

Talent management must be integrated into such activities and processes as budgeting, strategic planning and risk management.

Responsibility for overseeing talent management and making sure that there is an adequate return on investment should ultimately lie with the top management team. Those in charge of the talent management function should report to a committee made up of senior managers from across the whole business, which should meet regularly to make sure that the talent plan stays closely linked to the strategic plan and direction, agree any changes to the talent plan, make decisions about high-level risks and issues and sign off investment decisions.

The role of the CEO

An important factor underpinning Olam's talent management strategy is the close involvement of the company's chief executive, Sunny George Verghese. He chairs the committee overseeing key appointments and meets newly recruited members of the company's talent pool every quarter. Bose explains:

> Our chief executive stresses that the key expectation he has of his leadership team is to deepen and propagate the culture that underpins our growth. Any manager who comes into the GATP attends a session that the CEO conducts over four days. The sessions are intense. They start at 8am and end at 7pm. The CEO takes them through the rationale of why we are in business, what are we for, what the future is like, what is the strategy and what are the values and how do we live them.

His example, according to Eric Olsen of Heidrick & Struggles, should be followed by everyone:

> We find that often the chief executive intervenes for a short period saying this talent function isn't working, we need to get smarter, we need to get it more aligned around strategy. I'll give it to one of the senior HR people by calling him or her head of talent – and then I'll go off and do the things I do.
>
> This HR-led, process-based approach fails because the chief executive is the missing link. He or she needs to get much more active in the ownership of the outcomes. You wouldn't see the chief executive abdicate his or her responsibility for finance or marketing – yet it often looks like they simply lob the ball to the head of talent and then walk away from the consequences. They need to stay involved.

The foremost champion of this view is Indra Nooyi, chairman and chief executive of PepsiCo. As she explained in a 2011 presentation to chief executives in Boston:

> How much time should we as chief executives spend moving talent management from the art that it has been to real science? I'm going to challenge all of you and say that if you are not spending at least 40% of your time on talent management you might well run into an issue about going forward ... It is hard to find the time but tell yourself that this is critical to the company's future.
>
> At PepsiCo, we are an engine for talent development. We embrace it and it also means that we have to constantly reinvent what we are doing ... So it would not come as a surprise to you that the first thing I did when I became chief executive in 2006 was to get started on my senior executive succession planning, not just the succession planning for the chief executive but for the entire senior management team.
>
> The first thing we did as the leadership team was to sit down and ask ourselves this most important question – "Where do we want to take PepsiCo over the next 10–15 years?" From this came PepsiCo 20–25, a blueprint that sets out alternative scenarios for the company to drive sustainable growth and top-tier financial performance.
>
> That blueprint in turn informed the skills that we need in order to move the company forward. Then what we did was to go a step further. For both ambitious goals, we identified 300 critical senior leadership goals that we thought would make or break our success. We then asked, "What are our pipeline needs?" We built in demand ratios and said that we needed to have one emergency successor for each job, and then two people in the one to three year timeframe and another three people in the four to six year timeframe.
>
> Every one of these 300 jobs has six people racked and stacked behind them. This means that we need 1,500 to 1,800 leaders in the pipeline. Not all of them will make it. Some will plateau. Some will fall short. Others will leave. Others will join. But we have to make sure that we always have a full pipeline of 1,500 to 1,800 people to fill these 300 critical positions.

For the last four years, I spent about 30% of my time on this group of potential C-suite successors.

The role of heads of talent

The role of the talent director is to consult and brief the senior management team regularly, with the aim of making sure that the talent strategy stays aligned with the business strategy and is adapted as the strategy changes, and that it is producing the desired results.

Becky Snow is global talent director at Mars, a global chocolate, confectionery and pet-care business. She describes her role as:

Setting a guiding, shaping strategy, then engaging the leadership and business units behind the essence and framework of that strategy so they can find their own way of tapping into it.

She also looks after what she describes as the "infrastructure of talent management", which is the tools, processes and competency framework used by her team of regional talent directors. As part of her global role, Snow is responsible for succession planning for the top of the organisation, including their career development. However, she stresses:

One of our key roles is talent brokering to ensure there we keep our most promising managers visible and mobile across the business units. This mobility also helps prevent these units from becoming insulated in how they think and operate.

Much of Snow's time as talent director is spent talking to the company's business heads to make sure that they take responsibility for decisions made in their domains:

It is about encouraging the leadership to think more long term and this brings us to the most important shift we need to make, which is at all levels of the organisation to hold our associates (ie, staff) accountable to their responsibility to develop talent as a competitive differentiator.

Staying agile

The planners of talent strategies are facing a radically different set of circumstances than those confronted by their predecessors. Marielle de Macker, managing director of group HR at Randstad, observes:

The world is certainly changing and becoming more volatile ... It is therefore important to develop enough agility to respond in an appropriate way to this change but also to be able to predict what is coming – to see around corners. The challenge is not for talent managers to learn new tricks, tips and skills but to develop this raw capacity to see change coming and to develop the appropriate judgment about how best to respond.

A number of those interviewed for this book spoke of the need for firms to adopt a more agile approach that balances long-term planning with the ability to change direction quickly.

To be able to "lean into the future", HR staff need to strengthen their skills in strategic planning and become more adept at identifying the talent implications whenever there is a shift in strategy or the business environment changes. Scenario planning can help them do this, as can other "futuring" techniques used to question current assumptions and explore different models for the business and new ways of organising and performing highly skilled work.

At least once every two years there should be time set aside to anticipate how various new trends could affect the demand and supply of talent and the way skilled work could be organised. For example:

- innovations in technology;
- shifts in the external environment (using PESTLE – political, economic, social and technological, legal and environmental – analysis);
- corresponding changes in organisational structuring including delayering, reorganising and restructuring;
- changes in the business model, including mergers and takeovers, outsourcing and strategic partnerships;
- virtual working and flexible working;

- demographic trends, such as an ageing workforce;
- changing employee expectations about careers and employment.

Conclusion

The experiences of Unilever and Olam International illustrate the importance of recruiting and developing the right mix of high-calibre managers, leaders and specialists to support and grow their businesses.

Both companies have placed the highest priority on devising talent plans that reflect the priorities of the business. Talent managers have worked closely with operational managers to identify the capabilities that employees need if they are to deliver the business strategy. Their focus has been on the immediate operational needs of the business and the actions that will help deliver longer-term success.

An effective talent plan is closely tied to the company's strategic goals and priorities. Talent managers can undertake a rigorous assessment of the company's talent requirements in the short and medium term. But probably the most important factor contributing to an effective talent plan is the active involvement and support of the top management team, operational heads and other senior managers.

Few firms believe they have formulated agile talent strategies. Part of the problem is that HR managers need greater expertise in strategic workforce planning and other processes such as scenario planning.

However, a major barrier to HR playing a more strategic role is that talent management activities require much time and effort. The operational demands of talent management often leave little room for HR staff to think about wider issues. The greatest risk – and the greatest irony – is that in the effort to embed more rigorous and systematic talent management, firms may well be building systems that are too rigid for today's turbulent conditions. Chapter 3 looks at this issue in greater detail.

3 Managing the talent process

If you are not careful, you get so wrapped up in the process, turning the wheel, getting everything done, that you can completely forget the point of it. I see my goal being to lead the leaders to lead the talent. Therefore I try to focus on what's most important, what's most critical for the business, not on covering every person or role.

Becky Snow, global talent director, Mars

IN THE EARLY YEARS of this century, Nokia, a multinational communications and information technology company based in Finland, had an enviable reputation as a magnet for some of Europe's best and brightest engineers and managers. But in 2006, it introduced a new strategy, aimed at creating a reliable pipeline of talented people who could occupy roles within senior and middle management that had a critical impact on its performance.

Nokia had previously relied on fairly informal processes for identifying such roles within the organisation. However, the leadership team decided the company needed to be more systematic about how it defined these roles so it could groom people to fill these positions.

Regular workshops were held at which managers of each business unit worked with the HR team to look at their business goals and leadership capabilities, and a "talent map" was introduced using a nine-box grid to identify performance and potential (see Figure 1.1). Those with "star potential" in the upper right box were steered towards experiences and job assignments that would help prepare them for a more critical role in the future.

Nokia developed a "return on investment" matrix to help it quantify the potential benefits and risks of moving individuals into new, more stretching roles. The four quadrants mapped risk of failure against potential impact. Managers could then map the result against the cost of the individual's development.

This analysis was designed to make sure that the most money for personal development was allocated to managers who could potentially make a big impact in a role but who ran a high risk of failing. To give these managers the best chance of success, "a strong transition plan and support" were put in place. Nokia hoped that this risk-based approach would encourage managers to apply for more challenging roles and business leaders to give these individuals a chance to prove themselves.

The new approach for measuring performance and potential was adopted across the international business in line with Nokia's "egalitarian" culture, which gave business units considerable discretion on how to implement talent management. An internal review conceded, however, that while managers were clear about the competencies needed for a critical role, they were less clear about how to define potential. Cultural differences across regional units also influenced decisions about who was marked out as a rising "star".

Nokia's approach to talent management was well thought through but did not work. By 2011 it was clear that it had failed to understand how the market for mobile devices had shifted. Rivals like Apple and Samsung seized Nokia's dominant share of the market, while Stephen Elop, the new chief executive, in an infamous leaked memo, admitted that the firm "fell behind, we missed big trends and we lost time".

Elop's verdict was that Nokia had failed to adapt to a very different and intensely competitive marketplace. The firm continued to do the wrong things very well. Elop says:

> We poured gasoline on our own burning platform. I believe we
> have lacked the accountability and leadership to align and direct the
> company through these disruptive times.

He also pointed to a lack of collaborative ability, a quality that the firm urgently needs if its strategic partnership with Microsoft is to succeed against the "ecosystems" built by Apple and Samsung (see Chapter 6).

The Nokia example is a cautionary tale for business leaders and the managers that develop their best people. However large and well-oiled the machine for bringing on these people, it will fail to deliver the right results unless it also instils the need to keep a watchful eye on the bigger picture.

Processes and pipelines

As earlier chapters have outlined, a decade of talent management has led to many international companies focusing on the option of "building" a small number of high-flyers over several years. The mantra of the processes involved has been consistency, compliance and standardisation across international and global businesses.

This has arguably led to an industrial model of talent management, with concepts like talent "pipelines", "systems" and "infrastructure" becoming common parlance. The goal is to help gain an end-to-end view of talent management, but there is a tendency to think of talent more as a commodity rather than people who need to be trained and developed in ways that are individually tailored.

A strength of the model has been that it has brought professionalism and thoroughness to a process of selection and development that is otherwise prone to nepotism or cronyism and a tendency for managers to recruit successors in their own images. It has drawbacks, however. Organisations can become locked into a potentially narrow and rigid set of definitions of talent and potential and a management system that becomes increasingly complex and unwieldy as it develops a life of its own.

Eric Olsen at Heidrich & Struggles believes that HR staff are particularly prone to a tendency to construct overly complex talent programmes:

> In the FTSE 100 companies we studied, we saw a drive towards process. The only way these directors feel they can make an impact is to get involved with process, TM becomes a tight path of HR procedures, competency frameworks, etc. Yes, these are nice processes but they often don't really address the broader issues.

Roselinde Torres, senior partner and managing director at Boston Consulting Group, also highlights the need for HR to help develop more "customised" approaches:

Talent management is no longer about one size fits all. When you consider developed as opposed to developing markets, you need different types of leadership and you need to reconfigure your talent, especially in areas like research and development.

There needs to be a move towards a more customised and streamlined approach. In the absence of this, HR conducts a tremendous amount of activity with very little result.

Other managers overseeing talent management concur. David Smith of Accenture thinks that many companies have dug themselves into an administrative pit. As he puts it:

A lot of companies are stuck in a HR, administration led view of talent management. They tend to work in deep functional segments like performance management, recruitment and compensation. They need to take a more strategic view and look at the whole question of how they are going to attract and recruit talent into the organisation.

Becky Snow is well aware of this danger for a global business like Mars. She describes talent management variously as a big "tanker" and a "big machine". She warns:

If you are not careful, you get so wrapped up in the process, turning the wheel, getting everything done, that you can completely forget the point of it.

There is also the danger that talented people get lost in this machine and begin to feel undervalued and ignored by the organisation. This is particularly true for younger staff, as Sandra Schwarzer, director of careers services at INSEAD, an international business school based in France, reports:

Organisations that recruit MBA talent are often very strong on finding the right individuals and selling their organisations to them. But where they fall down is that once these individuals are on board, [there is not enough thought] about what happens to them.

Some of our alumni, for example, go on rotational programmes and get great experience, great exposure to the company's operations. But often after about three years, they feel like they are on their own ... Talented people are often left inside the different business units and get lost.

According to Snow, it is important to stop trying to build a perfect system.

I see my goal being to lead the leaders to lead the talent agenda. Therefore I try to focus conversations with our leadership team on what's most important, what's most critical for the business, not on discussing every person or every role.

New complexities and challenges

The old rules for talent management focused on standardisation and simplification; the new rules are intended to help companies adapt to change. Interviews carried out for this book suggest that companies are rethinking three aspects of their talent strategy:

- **A broader view of talent.** There is growing evidence that firms are no longer focusing exclusively on a small group of high-flyers who will become the next generation of executives. Companies are looking for a more diverse set of talented leaders and specialists. They are turning to untapped sources of talent, both within the organisation and externally.

- **Redefining talent.** Companies are analysing what it means to be successful in their context and are redefining the skills, knowledge and qualities that constitute talent. The outcome is a variety of definitions of what constitutes "talent" rather than the previously narrow view focusing on leadership succession.

- **Leveraging talent across the organisation.** The priority is to make sure that talented people are moved around the organisation, both to plug skill gaps and for personal development.

A broader view of talent

The traditional focus of talent management is on a small cadre of managers who are groomed to be the future leaders of a firm, focusing on succession planning as the main means to this end. However, this view of talent is too narrow for the many firms where the contribution of talented staff really does mean the difference between success and failure.

Often talented people are defined as those who have a disproportionate impact on the success of the business or who can generate significant added value (whether this takes the form of revenue, knowledge, reputation, and so on). The underlying principle is that the organisation needs talented individuals at all levels, not just at the very top.

Chapter 2 outlined how Olam International has gone through a transition in how it thinks about talent. As a result of its strategy of growth through vertical integration, the company has switched from needing general managers to needing "domain experts", leaders who can build new businesses in highly specialised fields. It has created two management groups or "streams" from which these roles can be filled:

- The country management stream consists of roles with direct responsibility for bottom line results for operations in local markets. Typical roles include regional controllers, country managers and profit centre managers.

- The functional stream consists of roles in areas such as finance and accounting, treasury and shipping, manufacturing and technical services. However, the focus is on organisation-wide abilities that can be applied across the organisation and applied internationally.

The people filling these roles are directly responsible for the profit and loss of a business or a section of businesses in more than one country. They are also part of a team of global business heads overseeing global strategy, resource allocation and logistics.

Olam has three talent pools to help fill these roles:

- The first, the global assignee pool, is for those individuals who are earmarked for global roles and who need to be exposed to international assignments.
- The second focuses on developing regional and national management teams.
- The third consists of graduate trainees.

Santander UK, a British bank wholly owned by the Spanish Santander Group, takes a similarly broad view of talent. It has expanded its definition of talent to include "exceptional functional and cross-functional talent" and has been piloting a talent assessment tool that reviews cross-functional/organisation skills, functional skills and a range of leadership skills linked to specific behaviours.

The bank pays a lot of attention to the development of young employees to support its rapid global expansion. The talent management team plans to recruit some 600 "early in career" individuals during 2014. These include apprentices, school leavers and university graduates.

As well as its graduate development programme, the bank has a "Flying Start" programme for school leavers to help them gain professional banking qualifications. It lasts for four years and is marketed as a "paid alternative to university". Selected school leavers go through induction and are assigned both a mentor and a buddy from their workplace to help them during the programme. They receive professional training through a mix of classroom training, e-learning and work shadowing. Participants progress through a series of professional qualifications, culminating in becoming a chartered banker. At the end of the four years, they are assigned to a role as a team leader, sales specialist or technical specialist.

Santander UK is also seeking to scoop up talented people overlooked by its competitors, such as postgraduates or high-flying graduates who are in their first or second job.

Although it has invested considerable resources in overhauling its entire talent management system, directors at the bank still look for as yet unidentified sources of talent. Stephen Dury, managing director of strategy and market development, comments:

> *Whenever I have an innovative and challenging project, which is about changing the business and shaping the organisation, I look for intrapreneurs, those people that feel an individual responsibility for doing things better, who think differently and want to make a difference ... people who might not appear on our talent map but who you know fit the talent profile that is needed.*

Caroline Curtis, head of talent, succession and leadership development, is equally concerned about talent outside the core banking business of Santander UK. She comments:

> *My feeling is that there may be opportunity to cast our net further afield; looking at the talent that we have within some of our own internal support companies.*

The issue of looking for talent at the "periphery" of the organisation (part-time, contract and associate staff) is explored in more depth in Chapter 6.

Demographic change

As outlined in Chapter 1, an ageing workforce is forcing companies operating in the United States and western Europe to rethink their talent strategies.

Such is the predicament of 3M, a technology company with 19,000 employees in more than 30 countries, which has ambitious growth plans, intending to fill 4,300 positions by 2015. When the talent implications for its five-year business plan were examined, a number of serious skills gaps became apparent. It also realised that it might struggle to achieve its target for succession planning, given that its workforce was ageing (with a forecast average age of 46.5 years by 2015) and not enough younger managers were in the pipeline.

3M therefore broadened its definition of talent to include both technical and leadership skills and recognised the need to take a more flexible approach to differences of demographics and labour conditions within European countries. The newly created global

Centre of Expertise for Talent Solutions now works in partnership with the country/region board of directors to fill their skills gaps through external recruitment and moving high-potential individuals around the business. Internal mobility has tripled since the new talent management processes were implemented.

In a 2012 report on talent mobility by the World Economic Forum, 3M advises that companies need to focus on a more tailored approach to developing people with talent:

> *Organisations must move from "one size fits all" tactics. Increasing workforce diversity means human capital planning must be innovative ... regional management teams should be flexible regarding talent mobility, leadership styles and generational differences.*

Wells Fargo, a multinational banking and financial services company, has taken a different approach to capitalise on the skills of both older and young workers. In some parts of the business, especially in the Great Lakes region of the United States, more than 50% of the workforce is under 30. In other regions, notably Indiana and Minnesota, there is a larger proportion of older staff. The company wanted to improve career-development opportunities for both these groups of employees, so the talent management group launched two internal networks, which are sponsored by senior managers and have dedicated resources to develop and engage them (see below).

Wells Fargo

Wells Fargo, one of the largest companies in the United States based on revenue, recognised that many of its older employees were likely to be forced to delay their retirement as a result of economic circumstances. It wanted to find a way to keep these employees motivated and engaged in their own career development.

In 2009 the talent management group launched an internal network for those born between 1946 and 1964, the "Boomers Network", which focuses on providing career-development opportunities for older workers and helps them deal with issues such as caring for elderly parents that might be affecting their well-being or career prospects. The company believed that older workers were being overlooked because of the stereotypical assumption that they were not interested in furthering their careers.

Wells Fargo already has approximately 52 internal networks in the Great Lakes region. These "Team Member Networks" represent specific groups of employees based on culture, ethnicity and sexual orientation. Each group must gain executive approval and enlist an executive sponsor, officers and chairs. The networks are allocated a budget and must submit annual plans detailing how they will provide opportunities for professional development, education and awareness, community service, as well as how they will benefit the business in any of the following five areas:

■ business development and customer insight;

■ team member engagement;

■ talent leader development;

■ community development;

■ branding and communication.

The effectiveness of the networks is assessed, using measures such as satisfaction scores of participants, growth of participation in the networks and how they have helped develop leaders, as are their business benefits, such as insights on customer preferences or feedback about new products.

Soon after the creation of the Boomers Network, young employees asked for a similar arrangement. So the Young Professional Network, which provides career development for employees aged below 30, was formed.

Members of both networks have worked with Wells Fargo's talent management group to look at how they can become more effective leaders. Courses in partnership with St Catherine's University were set up, some of which are offered on site at Wells Fargo and others on-campus. One programme, for example, leads to a graduate certificate in organisational leadership that can also count towards a degree in the same subject. There is also a leadership perspectives course, designed for baby-boomers, which aims to build on the experiences and leadership of people who want to develop their leadership skills in both their work and their personal life. Participants can opt for a life coach, although they have to contribute towards some of the costs of coaching.

Both networks have run a series of seminars looking at career development and other work–life issues, such as successful mid-life career changes, networking, managing money, healthy lifestyles and retirement planning.

Wells Fargo is now considering offering older employees more opportunities for part-time work, and is including health and wellness in its diversity and work–life programmes for all employees.

The talent management group looks at networks as both sources of talent and an ideal way to develop leaders. Each network is assigned two executive "advisers", who are chosen from the company's pool of high-potential talent. They then select the president of each network who puts together the network organisation. The advisers also set up meetings with senior managers to discuss business plans and how the networks can contribute; and senior managers may ask the networks for help on specific projects.

Diversity

An increased desire for diversity also demands that talent management become more flexible and customised.

A more diverse customer base has highlighted the need for companies to reflect greater diversity at every level of the organisation, not just at the top. In an analysis of this trend, Jean-Michel Caye and Karen Hinshaw, consultants at Boston Consulting Group, assert:

> Companies staffed exclusively with similar-looking, like-minded employees lack the broad range of insight and experience needed to meet the challenges of a globalising world. By contrast, organisations that tap into the full spectrum of capabilities of a diverse workforce are better equipped for a dynamic environment.

They say that managing a more diverse spread of talented people will pose challenges for firms, creating the need to modify the incentives they offer employees to meet more varied expectations. Mobility and regular feedback, for example, matter more to the latest generation of workers than they did to their older counterparts.

An *Economist* survey on diversity in 2011 reveals that while many firms acknowledge the benefit of developing more diverse senior leaders, such diversity is hard to achieve. Indra Nooyi does not feel that PepsiCo has cracked this particular nut:

How do we get people to embrace multi-generational, multi-cultural and multi-ethnic talent – and get people to walk in their shoes? Tough questions.

Despite the difficulties, she urges firms:

[To] leverage and integrate diversity. I'm talking about diversity of thought, background, experience, capability, culture, race, gender and also age diversity.

PepsiCo equates diversity in the way people think and act with a greater emphasis on recruiting and developing external talent:

Talent management requires courage, because outside points of view can shock inside talent ... they stretch us in terms of our thinking because many of us get locked into a traditional model and outsiders ask us whether we are wearing "Emperor's clothes". That makes a huge difference.

Age diversity in the top team is also desirable to PepsiCo, as Nooyi points out:

Too often at the top, everybody in that group tends to be of the same age group, even though we are dealing with technologies that we have never heard of. Yet we feel very uncomfortable when someone who is 10–15 years younger joins a senior team. We live in very unsettling times, but if we don't encourage age diversity at the top, I think our models might become outdated.

Spotting and accelerating the development of a young manager is not easy, so some firms have resorted to "reverse mentoring", where young people with a fresher view of the market counsel their elders. As the example of Boeing reveals, bringing together different generations of employees can result in powerful benefits both for individuals and the organisation.

Boeing

Multinational aerospace and defence corporation Boeing was concerned about both the loss of expertise as older workers approached retirement and the need to retain and motivate young "generation Y" workers, who represent the future workforce.

The company wanted to improve collaboration between these two groups of employees and to help them learn from each other. It especially wanted to help older workers become more confident with technology-based collaboration tools, and younger employees who were technically oriented to become better "people managers" and improve their communication and collaborative skills, especially using conversation as a means of problem solving.

Boeing piloted an approach to bring together generation Y employees and experienced managers in a "Workplace Innovation Lab". In 2009, it asked REACH (a network for early-career Boeing employees) members and their managers to seek volunteers to participate in the project. Managers and younger employees were asked to work together in pairs and commit to spending 24 hours over three months, including two face-to-face workshops, on achieving a business goal or project of their choice. Over the next ten weeks, they participated in a series of conference calls to discuss new ideas and approaches that could help Boeing improve the three areas they had chosen:

- virtual collaboration, using new technology, including social media;
- agile working, using alternative employment contracts and flexible working to build responsiveness and reduce fixed costs;
- building a culture of trust and engagement to improve productivity and encourage staff to develop their skills and adopt new ways of working.

Participants also attended a 24-hour "Innovation Event", an intensive programme of theory and practice in relation to affecting change and innovation. The final stage was to demonstrate the results of the project to Boeing's global head of HR. The experiment was judged to be highly successful and some valuable ideas were generated, leading to improvements and cost savings.

Managers and younger employees reported benefits from two-way mentoring; for example, older managers felt more confident about using collaboration tools such as web X, share point, global conference calling, webcams and Insite, Boeing's internal social-networking site. There was improved communication between the two groups, and both recognised the value of combining seasoned experience with a fresher and sometimes more questioning perspective.

Boeing plans to repeat the innovation labs but with one important difference. Instead of drawing together a wide variety of participants from across the whole organisation, it will aim for a critical mass of participants from a single business area. It believes this concentrated approach will generate more focused and measurable business benefits.

Cisco UK & Ireland, part of Cisco Systems, a multinational designer and manufacturer of networking equipment, also uses reverse mentoring for strategic planning. Small groups of generation Y employees (broadly, those born between 1980 and 2000) meet the senior management team regularly to discuss emerging trends which might pose both opportunities and threats to the business.

Reverse mentoring is part of a wider effort at Cisco UK & Ireland to build a broader and more diverse culture. It has been particularly successful at using mentoring and other schemes to attract and develop women. Indeed, its chief executive, Phil Smith, won "Mentor of the Year" at the Women of the Future Awards 2010 for his efforts in making the company an attractive employer to women.

Smith says that when he first started at Cisco's new country operation for the UK and Ireland in 1994, the fledgling company was "mainly middle-aged males". Its workforce of approximately 4,000 is now one of the *Times* Top 50 Places Where Women Want to Work.

The company's success is based simply on "listening to your employees" and being responsive to their individual needs, Smith says. There are many issues that are minor to solve for the company, but make a huge difference to staff, particularly work–life balance. Smith believes that a business must reflect the diversity of its customers and society at large, and that without that diversity it will lack dynamism; but he is also of the view that it must never be about fulfilling quotas. As he explains:

This is not good for an individual or a company. You need the best people for the job, and you as a company need to be doing the best for them.

However, despite extensive efforts among firms to get more women into senior management positions, few are succeeding. The reasons are examined in greater depth in the next chapter, but two reports highlight the problem.

A 2012 report by McKinsey, "Unlocking the full potential of woman at work", reveals that women may be well represented in junior management but many fail to progress to top management roles because they are either sidelined into staff jobs, get stuck at middle management, or leave the corporation. In terms of four "success" measures for getting women to the top (for example, having at least 55% of women vice-presidents and senior vice-presidents) only 12 of the 60 companies surveyed met three of the four measures.

A similarly dismal picture is painted by Catalyst, an American non-profit research organisation, which produced a report in 2010 based on the career-path profiles of 9,927 alumni who graduated between 1996 and 2007 from MBA programmes at 26 business schools in Asia, Europe, the United States and Canada, and additional data from 4,143 women and men who graduated from full-time MBA programmes and worked full-time at companies and firms at the time of the survey.

Sponsored by corporations that include American Express, Barclays Capital, IBM, Chevron, Procter & Gamble and Deloitte, the report pointed out that although women represented 40% of the worldwide workforce, few of them reach senior management positions (the results of this research are discussed in greater depth in Chapter 4). James S. Churley, chairman and CEO of Ernst & Young, a multinational professional services firm and a sponsor of the research, admits:

Frankly, the fact that the pipeline is not as healthy as we'd thought is both surprising and disappointing. Companies have been working on this, and I thought we'd seen progress. The last decade was supposed to be the "promised one" and it turns out that it wasn't.

This is a wake-up call for corporations. First, we need to put more pressure on business schools to coach women and men during the job placement process. Second, companies need to be looking at where women land when they come into the corporation. Then we need to make sure they're getting the same development and visibility chances as the men.

We need to focus even more on how we're leading our companies to get the most out of employees ... In this war for top talent we can't afford to do otherwise.

Diversity and business performance

In a survey of 656 business leaders in 2011, conducted by the Economist Intelligence Unit, diversity of gender, ethnicity and nationality is seen to be beneficial, but difficult to attain. The majority of respondents believe diversity in management:

■ helps promote the brand;

■ increases profitability;

■ deepens knowledge of new international markets.

Despite this belief, the vast majority of firms in the survey had no specific policy on diversity. A majority believed that the share of women and ethnic minorities in their global senior management is not fairly representative of their customers and markets. A plurality believes the same about foreign nationals.

The survey points to a connection between strong performance and greater diversity among executives. Among executives describing their firm's financial performance as "better than their peers", nearly half (47%) believe their board broadly reflects the gender, ethnic and nationality make-up of society. Only 27% of firms that are considered to perform "worse than their peers" claim this to be the case.

Talent in abundance

Whatever the difficulties involved, the message emerging from forward-looking companies is that organisations need an open mind and a broader approach if they are to tap into a wider set of abilities. They have to broaden their search to find talented individuals who might not fit traditional talent profiles. They need to have the courage to look outside for talented people who are willing to challenge entrenched thinking. Firms also need to "dig deep" into their own organisations to find talented individuals.

The great paradox of this new way of thinking is that it leads to a view that talent is abundant instead of a rarity – a view expressed in a report on global talent in 2009 by Tomorrow's Company, produced in partnership with Heidrick & Struggles, together with BT, Career Innovation and the UK government's Talent and Enterprise Taskforce. The report concludes:

> Today's competitive challenges require us to become very good at tapping into the talent we have, the full range and potential of it – what "Tomorrow's Global Talent" terms "the abundance" of it; building the skills that are needed and encouraging the creativity that is possible ... [Talent] is abundant in the sense that it is not a rare quality, but diverse and multifaceted, which everyone has, to some degree and in some form. And taking this view means that there is a wider pool of talent for companies to work with, if they know how to unlock it.

Redefining talent

Uncertainty lurks in today's business environment with change becoming less predictable, more disruptive and at an accelerating pace, which makes it all the more important that companies review on a regular basis the leadership and technical skills they need to be successful.

At Apple, every employee is expected to be innovative and to focus on product success rather than individual results. In pursuit of groundbreaking products, different teams may be assigned to the same product area and work in secrecy from each other. Innovation is stimulated through peer vetting of ideas and brainstorming to encourage bolder innovations and higher levels of risk-taking.

Mars has had a hard rethink about the qualities it needs to achieve its business plan. The company now looks for high performance and high potential in six areas. At the individual contributor level, it looks for the ability to deliver consistent results and to create collaborative relationships. For people leaders it adds engaging staff and developing talent. And for senior leaders it adds the ability to practise "breakthrough thinking" and to navigate complex challenges.

Mars's priorities are evident in Becky Snow's assertion:

> We are still working on all those capabilities but we have very good senior people. They are very good at collaborative relationships. They are not individualists. They are absolutely team players and they are very approachable as team leaders. This approachability is a core part of who we are as a business.

Apple and Mars have figured out what they need to do best to thrive in their very different contexts – and this has resulted in two very different sets of managerial and leadership abilities. The two companies have built an appropriate talent strategy around these capabilities, with Mars opting for a systematic, partnership-based approach to career development and Apple opting for few formal processes in favour of individuals managing their own career paths – which they do by networking and promoting their expertise so they get assigned to the most stretching projects.

According to Emily Lawson of McKinsey, too few companies achieve the clarity of Mars and Apple. They may well have ambitious plans and growth targets, but they have yet to spell out what this means for their talent strategies. She asserts:

> We find that lots of companies don't know what they are looking for. I had a typical conversation recently with a global organisation about its plan to expand its business in Asia. I asked them "in order to grow your markets, what do you need? Do you need great sales people, do you need very technical marketing people?" They didn't know. They just knew they wanted to grow 40% of their market.

The critical thing is to start from your business strategy and to be really clear about what talent you need and therefore where your gaps are – because they may not be where you think they are.

Interviews carried out for this book suggest that companies are rethinking their talent requirements across three dimensions: the first is the ability to move across different business models; the second is having the right blend of leadership, management and technical skills; the third is to be able to manage through uncertain or fast-changing business conditions.

Identifying the right leadership skills

BCG's research suggests that many firms are failing to adapt their leadership models quickly enough, as Torres explains:

> We have looked at the programmes, policies and practices used by global companies to develop their leaders. What we found is that, in headline form, most of those approaches were wired for leaders in the 20th century world rather than 21st century world.
>
> What we mean by that is that they presume more stability and less globalisation in [business] interactions. They don't account for the transparency and flow of information in a digital world. They tend to develop people in one business model or one geography.

BCG advocates the need for "adaptable leadership". This has four dimensions:

- **navigating ambiguous business environments** – mainly through cultivating a diversity of perspectives and sharing the lead with the individual or group best equipped to guide a specific decision;
- **leading with empathy** – through creating a shared purpose and managing through influencing;
- **leading through self-correction** – by insisting that individuals and teams learn through experimentation while still staying focused on business priorities;
- **creating win-win solutions** – by focusing on sustainable success for the companies and its shareholders, building

"collaborative platforms" and using "soft power" to ensure stakeholders' agendas stay aligned.

Rival consultancy McKinsey has gone down a different route. Instead of advocating a specific set of leadership traits, it has highlighted business context as the all-important ingredient.

McKinsey worked with Egon Zehnder, a global executive search firm, to identify the leadership traits that are most likely to deliver revenue growth. The research consisted of a statistical analysis of the relationship between managerial quality and revenue growth across a global sample of more than 5,000 leaders in 47 listed companies. The analysis was based on Egon Zehnder's eight-scale leadership framework.

The 2011 study confirmed the importance of outstanding leadership, as opposed to merely good leadership. However, the most important leadership skills depend wholly on the context in which a firm operates. The study concludes: "Talent matters: executives of high-growth companies have a higher level of competency than those of low-performing firms." But it also makes it clear that having good leaders is not good enough; only excellence makes the difference. Companies with outstanding leadership teams have a high correlation with revenue growth, while those with solid but unexceptional leaders have no correlation at all.

Beyond a focus on "customer impact", the analysis revealed that there is no standard skill set for success. Instead, companies need "spiky leaders". As Emily Lawson explains:

> When we say "spiky" we don't mean sharp-elbowed and edgy. We mean people with a clear spike in their performance so that they are exceptionally strong in two or three of the core leadership traits identified by the research.

The report advises: "Celebrate the extremes, develop and promote spiky leaders." Lawson adds: "This finding was contrary to what we expected. It hasn't been what we were advising to clients."

Uncertainty and turbulence

Whatever leadership skills work best for a company, managing uncertainty is becoming a crucial ability for senior managers responsible for deciding and implementing strategy.

Following its rapid growth, Standard Chartered, a British multinational banking and financial services company, has redesigned its leadership development and succession planning. It wants to develop more adaptable leaders and also prepare them for a much more complex environment where sudden shifts in politics, legislation or social attitudes can combine in unpredictable ways and force a rethink of strategy. It now operates in over 70 markets, and its leadership team grew by over 40% between 2009 and 2011, with almost two-thirds of new leaders coming from inside the bank.

Standard Chartered recognises that it cannot adopt a single model of leadership when its staff comprises 125 nationalities and managerial styles vary according to the specific culture and business situation faced by each business region. Simon Lau, head of the bank's leadership development programmes, says:

> You have to look at whether traditional Western leadership philosophies are going to work in the Middle East, for instance. What we do is to build leadership around the context.

Heather Ward, leadership succession manager, adds: "Leadership is distributed around the business, and it is a collaborative process."

The bank has put in place a comprehensive range of programmes to help nurture its leaders and managers, from external hires at director level to those managing a small team. An important learning module for all leaders covers leadership in turbulent times. Lau explains:

> Our leaders need to be comfortable anticipating and dealing with change. This module covers the skills leaders need in such circumstances. They need to be able to focus their people, communicate, involve them in the problem and empower them to take some ownership of how to solve it.

Formal leadership training is supported by on-the-job learning. All leaders receive one-to-one coaching and team support, which is provided by in-house leadership coaches.

Tata Chemicals, a global company based in India, has found that in its Asian operations young, ambitious employees become frustrated and anxious when they cannot easily make decisions in the face of ambiguous or contradictory data. This has sometimes caused them to leave the organisation. Helping these youngsters to cope with these pressures is crucial. Budaraju Sudhakar, chief human resources officer, explains:

> When we are putting youngsters into challenging positions, their ability to manage their own confusion and anxiety is becoming a very big issue. We are spending a lot of time building their ability to do this. Helping them develop emotional intelligence is a priority for us.

The company focuses on helping young managers develop more realistic goals and to develop the right "attitude, humility and respect" to thrive in uncertainty or difficult work environments. The company also works with senior leaders to "create a mindset of nurturing the organisation," says Sudhaker.

Focus on people, not abilities

Where does this leave a company's talent strategy if its leadership requirements are unclear or in the process of shifting, and where the very definition of outstanding leadership is heavily determined by the context in which it is applied? The answer is arguably to focus on the underlying attributes that help make a high-flyer adaptable in the face of uncertainty and change. These often include self-awareness, resilience and the ability to learn rapidly.

For example, Ian Pearman, chief executive of Abbott Mead Vickers, an advertising agency, says that personal commitment is more important than ability for his company. He maintains:

> You hire for attitude and you train for skill. That is dead right. If the definition for performance is capability plus commitment, you train for capability. The degree of commitment or drive comes from within. While we offer to enhance everybody's capability equally, the thing that creates the difference is people's level of commitment.

Marielle de Macker, HR managing director at Randstad, has reached similar conclusions. Whether leadership or expert talent, the latter of which is fast becoming a priority for the company (as a result of more complexity in labour legislation and different labour-market conditions), the company focuses on three personal attributes:

> When I think about talent, I think about three things. First, I think about drive – does somebody have the drive and the energising skills to encourage people to go the extra mile.
>
> Second, I think about judgment – the world is no longer black and white and you will have to formulate decisions based on incomplete and conflicting information and data. What is required is expertise and experience as well as intelligence and a highly developed sense of integrity.
>
> Third, I think of courage – you need to be prepared to take a position and defend it, not to the level of insanity obviously but people are looking for someone to lead them. People want leadership. You need the courage to be able to stand up for your beliefs, to stand up for your company, to stand up for your people and go for it.

McKinsey's Emily Lawson endorses this message:

> Our research shows that companies are pretty much focusing on the same leadership traits; they are just calling them different things.
>
> I would probably not put my investment in finding the right leadership model. I think companies should spend their money on discovering what kind of people they need to deliver the business.
>
> I think you should spend your money on having a really robust employee value proposition that is tailored to the different markets in which the business needs to operate. What works for a graduate in China is not going to work for a senior banker in Dusseldorf.

Leveraging talent across the business

The ability to move talented people across the business has become critical for international companies, both to use and deploy talent more effectively and to make sure that these individuals gain sufficient exposure to different operating environments.

A 2010 report into talent mobility by PriceWaterhouseCoopers, a multinational professional services firm, highlights the importance of moving talent. As well as an increasingly globally connected world, "an explosion of activity in emerging markets has contributed to a significant increase in the need for companies to move people and source talent from all around the world."

Based on a variety of data, PriceWaterhouseCoopers reports that the number of international assignments increased by 25% between 1998 and 2009. It predicts a further 50% growth in assignments by 2020. There will "especially be more quick, short-term and commuter assignments". The research also points to the growing importance of emerging markets and the likelihood that skilled employees from these regions will become increasingly mobile, "creating greater diversity in the global talent pool".

Mars is already grappling with the challenge of making its talent more mobile and is especially keen for its best-performing leaders in emerging markets to have opportunities to move across the business. The company recognises that it will need to differentiate more if it is to channel resources into parts of the company that are growing most rapidly. Strategic workforce planning is becoming increasingly important in making sure that there is enough of the right talent in the parts of the business that are growing most rapidly. Mars also recognises that talented managers within these centres of growth need to get more international experience, and that it needs to focus on spotting and developing talented professionals who originate in centres of the company's growth like Asia. As Becky Snow explains:

> We decided to stop trying to pay equal attention to every role and every succession plan, which in the past meant we spent about 30 seconds on each individual. The new priority in our reviews is to pick a handful of key people and learn more deeply about them to support their development.
>
> Mobility is a real challenge. When we recently looked at the way we invest in international moves, we found that the majority of the assignees come from mature markets. We want to balance this investment better towards our talented managers in our growth markets.

IBM, a multinational technology and consulting corporation, has decided to focus on younger employees who have been identified as "emerging leaders", instead of sending senior managers on international assignments. Not only were such assignments becoming increasingly expensive, but only a limited number of managers could take up these opportunities. Now the company aims to provide formative experiences much earlier in managers' careers so that they can experience the reality of working in global markets.

IBM's goal is to become a genuinely global firm, not an American company with outposts around the world. Robin Willner, former vice-president, global community initiatives, set up the new approach. He explains:

> We needed to begin to work with emerging leaders as well as our existing leadership core to become leaders in a global economy, adept and skilled at doing business in every and any kind of market, and understanding how to lead teams that included "IBMers" who could be in any of 170 countries.

Approximately 500 emerging leaders a year are sent in teams of 8–15 all over the world to spend four weeks working on a real business project. Each team typically comprises individuals from more than ten different countries. They spend three months preparing for the posting, learning about, for example, building a virtual team, the global economy, global leadership, corporate citizenship and, particularly, the growth market where they will be deployed.

The pre-work is geared to help teams "hit the ground running," says Willner. Team members work on a wide variety of tasks, ranging from supply chain management to implementing an HR policy or a new customer relationship management (CRM) system. IBM eschews Western-style hotels in favour of local accommodation to give the team an authentic experience of working abroad as well as getting along with a diverse group of colleagues. Willner believes this experience is succeeding in giving younger managers a more global and informed outlook:

> They learn about leadership and teaming and diversity and how to listen and learn how to do business somewhere else. They also learn a lot about themselves.

Procter & Gamble

Procter & Gamble (P&G), a multinational consumer-goods company, is a classic example of a company that has adopted a "build" approach to attracting and retaining talent. It adopts a cradle-to-grave philosophy. Over two-thirds of its leaders were recruited as university graduates and it was in one year able to attract about 600,000 applicants worldwide – of whom it hired about 2,700 – by emphasising opportunities for long-term careers and promotion from within. The website targeted at potential recruits states:

Our success depends entirely on the strength of our talent pipeline, which we build from within and manage with a disciplined process led by the CEO and the senior leadership team.

P&G has established a plethora of elaborate systems and processes to deploy talent. It has tied its talent management processes to its strategy for growth, which means a focus on winning in the emerging markets of China, India, Latin America, the Middle East and eastern Europe. The company is building what amounts to a global talent supply chain management process, co-ordinated worldwide but executed locally. Hiring and promotions are the responsibility of local managers, but high-potential prospects and stretching assignments are identified globally.

New hires tend to be local talent. Line managers in China, for instance, hire Chinese recruits. The days when managerial roles in emerging markets usually went to expatriates are past. Now, local hires are considered growth prospects for the firm and are expected to become managers in that market. Stretching assignments and senior positions, however, are managed by the global HR group and overseen by the global executive team.

The emphasis on hiring local people helps create a more diverse pool of talent for the entire corporation, especially at more senior levels: 300 or so senior regional and country managers come from 36 countries, with 50% from outside the United States; the top 40 come from 12 different countries, with 45% from outside the United States.

As high-potential employees advance, they move through a portfolio of senior-level jobs that are categorised according to strategic challenges, size of the business and complexity of the market. Leadership positions for businesses or countries are earmarked for either novice or experienced general managers.

A relatively small country-manager position – in Taiwan, for instance – is considered appropriate for first-time general managers. Such assignments then set up the incumbents for placement in larger countries, such as Italy or Brazil, which in turn can lead to roles in clusters of countries, such as eastern Europe or the UK. These last roles then become springboards for leaders who demonstrate the potential to become senior managers.

P&G offers formal training and development programmes and sometimes enrols managers on external executive education programmes. The lion's share of development, however, takes place on the job, with the immediate manager's support and help from mentors and team members. A typical marketing manager, for example, will have worked with a number of different brands over a period of time. A finance manager will have gone through various assignments, ranging from financial analysis to treasury to auditing to accounting.

Most high-potential managers are also placed in important multifunctional task-forces or project teams from time to time. New postings and task-force participation are expected to challenge employees, and they signal to managers that P&G will always offer new opportunities.

People and positions are tracked in a technology-based talent management system that is sufficiently robust to accommodate all the company's more than 135,000 employees but is primarily used to track 13,000 middle- and upper-management employees. The system captures information about succession planning at the country, business-category and regional levels; includes career histories and capabilities, as well as education and community affiliations; identifies top talent and their development needs; and tracks diversity. It also makes in-house talent visible to business leaders, who no longer have to scour the company to find candidates by themselves.

To keep the system relevant, P&G has instituted a global talent review – a process by which every country, every function and every business is assessed for its capacity to find, develop, deploy, engage and retain skilled people, in the light of specific performance objectives. For example, if the company has stated diversity hiring objectives, the review is used to audit diversity in hiring and promotions. Determinations made in these reviews are captured in a global automated talent development system and can be accessed by decision-makers through their HR managers.

The processes used by P&G are well-established but the managers who run them are conscious of the way talent management is being transformed by changing demographics and the new demands of candidates from generation Y and women (see Chapter 4).

P&G's head of HR, Sonali Roychowdhury, argues that the processes adopted by the company are "social" as well as technical. As she concludes:

In the current scenario and increasingly becoming stronger there are three major trends that I see shaping the talent management space: one is the overall talent management approach moving away from the traditional "checking the box" approach of competencies to more a social process; second is the increasing importance of the use of technology specially as an integrator of all the functions in talent management; and finally the relevance of diversity in the talent management strategy going forward.

Talent management needs to be understood as both a formal and a social process. Traditionally competencies have been analysed following a formal structure and primarily focusing on final results. Currently it is a formal structure process, one-fits-all approach. Today, that cannot work any more; today we need to have a more targeted approach to be able to leverage the talent of different people and deselect those who do not fit a particular mould.

Results are of course important but how those results are achieved is becoming equally important; that's why I think talent management today is as much a social process. The softer aspects of talent management will be the differentiators in the future. In P&G we look at the numbers, the results, but also the way those are achieved. This focus on the process helps us identify skills that people have that otherwise could have been missed.

Our talent review process includes senior leadership, mentors, managers observing the individual in a series of assignments/situations (meetings, management interactions, accelerator experiences – often spanning years) from which they get intimate insights into "how" results are achieved (the context in which the results were delivered, influencing skills, peer interaction, collaboration across different cultures, social intelligence, ability to form and sustain productive networks internally, etc).

This is then converted into an actionable assessment of potential and destination roles that the individual would be a good fit for. This results in customised talent plans for individuals and finds a fit for different skills throughout the organisation.

Conclusion

In the past decade there has been growing use of a process-led approach to talent planning, focusing on a small cohort of high-flyers who are destined to become future top leaders. Such an approach works well when the business environment is relatively stable and companies are reasonably confident about their strategies and the capabilities to execute their plans successfully.

The benefit of an HR process-based "machine" is that it helps ensure consistency and a useful end-to-end view of how and where talent needs to enter and move across the organisation. The drawback is that it can become so resource intensive that companies spend too much time and energy on administration and operational issues rather than assessing whether it still supports the business strategy.

Companies in uncertain or highly competitive conditions are rethinking their approach to talent management. They are not necessarily dismantling their systems but are looking at the question of how to build in more flexibility.

They are reconsidering their talent requirements in the light of their strategic priorities and moving towards a broader view of talent. They are widening their focus beyond leadership succession to include technical and functional specialists and any individuals who have a "disproportionate" impact on business performance. These employees are increasingly required to have a complex set of skills and attributes in order to operate across different business models and different business contexts.

International companies, especially those with growth ambitions, need their talented staff to be highly mobile. To guarantee that talented individuals have both sufficient depth and width of experience, companies are resorting to longer-term career paths.

This is a tall order for talent planning and it presupposes that talented people are willing to be developed and deployed at the whim of the company. This may not necessary be the case.

Companies cannot afford to presume that they "own" their talent. Nor can they treat talent like a commodity or lump their most valuable employees into an amorphous "pool" of talent. Instead, they need to take a more tailored approach and work with talented individuals to agree a career path that benefits both parties.

The next chapter looks at how companies can take a more tailored and differentiated approach to their most valuable employees.

4　The individual and the organisation

One of the things that surprises me is the number of times the net generation, born after 1980, comes up in the conversation – and that it has higher expectations and wants the opportunity to be mobile. But to what extent is this generation different? I think we are very often talking about aspects of organisational life that are important to an increasingly large proportion of our employee base. Increasingly, all our employees are demanding more focus, doing meaningful work and having greater autonomy.

Jon Ingham, human resources and organisation
development consultant

OUT OF TALENT MANAGEMENT CONFERENCES and summits the world over has come the conclusion that certain categories of employees may not be willing to play the talent management game according to the current rules.

Attention has focused on two groups in particular: generation Y, otherwise known as the net generation or millennials and broadly defined as those born between 1980 and 2000, who may not have the patience to play the waiting game required to reach the top of organisations; and women, who either face additional barriers to promotion than their male counterparts or are not prepared to pay the personal price required of aspiring senior managers.

Indra Nooyi, chairman and CEO of PepsiCo, says the "evolving expectations" of these two groups of employees are at the top of her list of challenges for talent management:

Millennials – they want more flexibility. They talk about career lattices, not ladders. They want challenges of major proportions early in their lives. They want autonomy, they want on-demand training and abundant recognition. If you look at all the needs they present to us, it is just exhausting.

She also points to the needs of women (and increasingly men too):

Globally, the number of highly educated women entering the workforce will overtake men in the next five years. That is a pretty profound change. Men and women today are expecting more time for their personal lives. Dual careers, working mums and ageing parents – I don't think we can ignore those trends any more because they are very real when we think about how to manage our people to keep companies successful.

The problem is that the bar has raised and we need to clear the bar to reach the super-talented next generation to keep companies moving forward.

This chapter aims to sift the truth from the ocean of assumptions made by researchers and commentators about the real needs of women and members of generation Y, to examine the extent to which these needs are really different from those of the rest of the labour force (in the sense that a growing proportion of their colleagues share their scepticisms about the talent game and also the need for a corporate helping hand) and to highlight the implications for career planning and personal professional management as it is currently practised.

Generation Y: separating fact from fiction

Members of generation Y are sometimes portrayed as lazy, selfish, immature and overly dependent on their parents, leading to labels like the "me first" generation and the "tethered generation". More positively, they are hailed as "digital natives", whose technological savvy ensures they use technology and social networks for every aspect of their personal and working life.

In the United States, some 80m people belong to generation Y. Globally, it is estimated that they number around 3.6 billion, making up nearly half of the world's population. It is estimated that by 2025, three out of four workers globally will be from this generation.

Generation labels

Give or take a couple of years either side of the generation, the various generations have been grouped as follows:

- The millennial generation or generation Y: those born after 1980 and the first generation to come of age in the new millennium.

- Generation X: those born between 1965 and 1980, originally called the "baby bust" because of falling birth rates.

- Baby-boomer: so named because of the spike in the birth rate in the West after the end of the second world war, beginning in 1946 and ending with the availability of the birth-control pill in 1964.

- The silent generation: adults born between 1928 and 1945 whose "silent" label refers to their conformist and civic instincts.

- The greatest generation: those born before 1928 who Ronald Reagan, an American president, famously said "saved the world" through fighting and winning the second world war.

Emily Lawson of McKinsey makes the point that while baby-boomers and people from generation X (see box) are in reality Western concepts and phenomena, the traits of people from generation Y are more global. She comments:

> Generation Y is the first one of these that you can start talking about globally. They do all know each other, they do talk to each other and they listen to broadly the same music. They surf the net and they play video games. They own the same technology.
>
> The one thing about generation Y is that they do have global expectations and global awareness, which would have been much harder for the baby-boomers to acquire at that age. They are also getting, in orders of magnitude, information about the world. I certainly think they have a different skill set in how they manage and distil information and in how they manage their lives.

Research by Ashridge, a UK business school, however, found that although many aspects of generation Y apply around the world, such as their focus on self, loyalty to their peers rather than respect for hierarchy, and a preference for a strong work–life balance, there are other areas where characteristics are more prevalent in one region rather than another. The 2012 report, *Culture Shock: Generation Y and their Managers Around the World*, concludes:

> *In India, technology is a strong driver of Gen Y in the work environment. In the Middle East, the multinational aspect of business combined with an increasing number of locals educated abroad and returning is affecting how Gen Y approaches work. In China, the one child policy has created a very strong view of a spoilt and cosseted generation.*
>
> *In the UK, a lack of career direction with frequent job experimentation and orientation towards "fun" at work is noticeable. In Malaysia, although more loyal to their companies than elsewhere, Gen Y seeks international experience and varied careers. None of these characteristics is unique to a geographical region. They apply everywhere, but have a stronger emphasis in different parts of the world.*

People from generation Y are a crucial section of the workforce in the West as the bulge group of "baby-boomers" born between 1943 and 1963 is beginning to retire. Although they will soon make up the greatest proportion of the workforce, there will be fewer of them from which to choose (compared with baby-boomers and generation X).

Nooyi says that any company doing the maths must have cause to worry:

> *Any way you look at it, if you are running a global enterprise today, you have got to worry about what talent is out there ... In the West, 75m baby-boomers are nearing retirement. There are only 30m Gen Xs coming up behind them. There is going to be a talent shortage.*

The technological prowess of people from generation Y is a trait that many companies are eager to harness, as Lucian Tarnowski, founder and chief executive of BraveNewTalent.com, argues:

> *Something that nobody can debate – and there are lots of debates about whether young people are naive and overambitious – is that*

*the youngest people entering the workplace today, for the first time
ever in history, are an authority on something that actually matters.
Young people are the authority on the internet, on social media, on
the change that this is bringing about.*

*Gen Y is living the change whereas when my parents graduated,
they were not an authority that mattered yet. The NetGen
understands the implications of technology and the daily use of
technology better than the CEOs of the organisations they are being
hired into. That has changed the playing field and changed the
workplace and the culture of the workplace.*

There is hard evidence to support the claim that the millennials
are at ease with technology, although the gap between them and
generation X is dwindling in some areas of technology use. A 2010
study by the Pew Research Center concludes:

*The internet and mobile phones have been broadly adopted in
America in the past 15 years, and millennials have been leading
technology enthusiasts.*

*For them, these innovations provide more than a bottomless
source of information and entertainment, and more than a
new ecosystem for their social lives. They also are a badge of
generational identity. Many millennials say their use of modern
technology is what distinguishes them from other generations.*

Shared concerns

Lifestyle priorities stated by people from generation Y interviewed in
the Pew Research Center report contradicts the "me first" label often
attributed to them (see Table 4.1).

Ashridge has also explored the validity of stereotypes about
people from generation Y through a survey of 692 respondents aged
between 16 and 63. The 2009 study, *Generation Y: Inside Out*, looked
at how older workers perceived individuals from generation Y as well
as how these young workers saw themselves. It concluded:

*Media hype has produced a largely untrue image of Gen Y, which
may be restricting their potential in the workplace and society.
Just like any other group of human beings, generation Y is made*

TABLE 4.1 **Lifestyle priorities of generation Y**

	%
Being a good parent	52
Having a successful marriage	30
Helping others in need	21
Owning a home	20
Living a religious life	15
Having a high-paying career	15
Having lots of free time	9
Being famous	1

Note: Based on the responses of 830 adults aged between 18 and 29.
Source: Pew Research Center, 2010

up of individuals. There are wide variations in their attitudes and behaviours.

All this evidence suggests that some of the praise and criticism surrounding people from generation Y is overblown and that organisations need to think more about them as individuals with their own specific values.

Great expectations

There is, however, compelling evidence to suggest that high-flying employees from generation Y have a set of attitudes and expectations that are not easy for organisations to accommodate.

Employees from generation Y, according to recent research, are ambitious and want challenging or exciting work, but they are not as willing as their parents to sign up for a demanding corporate career which might require long hours or personal sacrifice. Gaining their trust and loyalty also appears to be problematic. They are quick to leave the organisation if their needs (or demands) are not being met.

A study of graduates by Ashridge and the Institute of Leadership and Management (ILM) in 2009 certainly paints a picture of a generation with high expectations and a low tolerance level. People from generation Y expect much from work – and vote with their feet if employers fail to deliver. The graduate respondents in the study had a long list of complaints about how their experiences had fallen below their expectations (see Table 4.2)

TABLE 4.2 **Unmet expectations of graduates**

	%
Salary	45
Career advancement	38
Job status	30
Feeling valued and treated with respect	29
Doing work of value to society	29
Achievement in work	28
Challenging and interesting work	22

Note: Based on the responses of 1,222 graduate recruits.
Source: Ashridge and Institute of Leadership and Management, 2009

Nor do people from generation Y expect to be in one job or organisation for long. The study of American workers by the Pew Research Center describes workers from generation Y as "job hoppers" and says that, not surprisingly given the length of their working life, two-thirds of those surveyed expected to move on from their current employer, viewing their job either as a "stepping stone" to a career, or "just a job to help them get by". The report goes on to say:

Remarkably, nearly six in 10 employed millennials say they already have switched careers at least once, suggesting that many millennials are trying out different careers (or that some respondents equated a job change with a career switch).

The Ashridge/ILM study highlights its findings about graduate career intentions:

One of the most compelling findings [is that] over half (57%) of graduates expect to leave their employer within two years, with 40%

expecting to leave in one year. A surprisingly high 16% intend to go as soon as possible – more women (19%) than men (11%).

Of the respondents who intended to leave straight away, some 75% did not feel valued or that they were treated with respect, while 74% were disappointed about their job advancement.

As the study comments:

> The figures must be worrying for employers. From a purely financial perspective, high graduate turnover is a waste of resources ... Equally concerning, however, is the potential impact on developing long-term strategy, building an organisation's talent pool and cohort of future leaders and indeed on corporate competitiveness. If organisations wish to staunch this flow of talent, they will need to be proactive in taking steps to prevent such an exodus.

A later report from Ashridge in 2012 developed the theme.

> The biggest concern for the worldwide managers we interviewed is the issue of retention of young people. Compared to the past, they see that graduates have little patience with a job and will leave quickly if they feel it doesn't meet their own personal ideals ... Keeping graduates beyond the two-year mark is a key goal.

What do 21st-century workers really want?

So what do people from generation Y really want? What do employers need to do to engage this generation and make the most of their talents? Are their needs distinct or do they share some traits with older talented employees or women, who constitute another untapped source of talent in the workplace?

There are four dimensions of work which, although important to any and every employee, appear to be crucial in motivating and retaining people from generation Y and other talented individuals in the workplace: rapid job advancement; money and challenging work; work–life balance; and freedom and autonomy.

Rapid job advancement

Rajeeb Dey is the founder and chief executive of Enternships.com, an online enterprise aimed at connecting entrepreneurial university students to opportunities for internships within small and medium-sized businesses.

Dey is 28 and in 2012 was named a "Young Global Leader" by the World Economic Forum. Despite two internships at the Bank of England and Boston Consulting Group, both of which subsequently offered him a job, he opted for self-employment and has never looked back. He explains why he was not lured by these tempting job offers:

> I don't like bureaucracy and I don't like hierarchy. If I need something done, I want to do it myself and I don't want permission from a lot of people to make it happen. I think generally in corporate structures, but less so in consulting, you have to go through the rigmarole of being an analyst or an associate and climb your way up to the next stage as part of a very linear career progression that doesn't work for me. I felt that in my nature I would be frustrated.

Dey is not alone in being frustrated by the prospect of slowly climbing up the corporate ladder. A 2008 study by Robert Half International, an American human resource consulting firm, and Yahoo! Hotjobs, an online job search engine, reveals that 51% of respondents believed they should spend only 1-2 years "paying their dues in entry-level positions" before progressing. A further 16% believed this period should be less than one year. When asked how long they planned to stay in their current position, 16% said less than one year and 24% between one and two years.

The 2009 Ashridge/ILM study paints a similar picture. Graduates expect rapid career progression, especially into management roles. Despite previous research by the ILM showing that most managers are not appointed until their early 30s, 32% of the graduate respondents are aiming to obtain a management role by at least the end of their second year of working (compared with 23% of managers who think this is realistic). Some 13% think they should reach these roles by the end of their first year at work (compared with 6% of managers who share that view).

As the study comments:

This highlights that graduates' expectations of a rapid rise to management are ambitious and pose a potential challenge for organisations and their managers.

When considering how long graduates should work before being promoted into their first management role, research by Ashridge in 2012 found there were differing views. Graduates in the UK and the Middle East said "within 2–3 years"; in Malaysia and India 4–5 years was considered reasonable. However, 12% of Malaysian and Indian and 14% of UK graduates indicated a period of less than one year. Across the world about 20% said that it depended on the individual.

Well-designed training schemes can help move promising graduates around the organisation to gain a variety of experiences, but they can sometimes cause even further frustration and disappointment.

As Sandra Schwarzer, director of career services at INSEAD, explains:

Companies are very good at selling their organisation to talented graduates, but then they fall down once these people are on board. Some of our alumni, for example, tell us they initially got great experience through a job rotation programme, great exposure to the company's operations. But after this, they say they felt like they were on their own. These people are still in need of a career track and want to know where they will stand in three or five years' time.

However, older managers can feel similar frustrations, according to Claire Lecoq, director of MBA admissions, marketing and careers services at IMD, a business school based in Switzerland. IMD's MBA programme is typically made up of middle managers with an average age of 31, many of whom quit their organisations to study for an MBA. Lecoq explains:

In our current group of 90 MBA students, 87 quit their former organisation, although pretty much two-thirds of them had the option to return.

Even when their organisations want them back, graduates can end up leaving. As Lecoq concludes:

Organisations are sometimes not organised internally to exploit the potential of that person. They may not support the individual properly when they return by exploring opportunities with them – so they get frustrated and leave.

A 2010 Catalyst report suggests that high-flying MBA graduates are indeed lured away by better career opportunities elsewhere. The study found:

- the main reason women and men left their first post-MBA job was for faster career advancement, men more so than women;
- more men than women said they left to earn more money or receive better benefits;
- men and women left to make a career change at equal rates.

A study in 2010 by the UK's Chartered Institute of Personnel and Development (CIPD) looked at the experiences of 310 senior leaders included in their organisation's talent programme. Asked to rank their reasons for participating, 54% said they hoped that it would help them to progress faster in the organisation. However, looking at their experiences after the programme, only 13% of the senior leaders believed they had achieved a promotion sooner than would have been the case if they had not participated.

This suggests a degree of disappointment among those leaders. In follow-up interviews with a small number of them, the CIPD notes that some gave "frank warning" of the danger of developing senior leaders "only for them to discover that the opportunities they had hoped for within their own organisations were not available".

Companies are also struggling to make sure that the career progression of high-potential women keeps pace with that of their male counterparts. Research by McKinsey in 2012 reveals that "young women, just like young men, start out with high ambitions" but that, for a variety of reasons, "the end result is that the odds are consistently stacked against women climbing higher at every step of the career ladder – not just at the top".

The McKinsey report says that women lose out at every level of the organisation. Although many more companies now recruit a significant proportion of women, they become increasingly underrepresented as they move higher up the organisation (see Table 4.3).

TABLE 4.3 **Representation of women in management**

	Average % of women
Whole company	37
Middle management	22
Senior management	14
Executive committee	9
Chief executive	2

Note: Based on 130 European companies with more than 10,000 employees.
Source: McKinsey & Company, 2012

Many of the same questions are asked about women's hunger for top jobs as are asked of people from generation Y; indeed, at a Society for Human Resource Management conference in 2009, Jack Welch, former chief executive of General Electric, provoked a storm of protest when he said:

> There's no such thing as work–life balance ... we would love to have more women moving up faster. But they have got to make the tough choices and know the consequences of each one.

Welch provoked further controversy at a *World Street Journal* conference in 2012 when he reiterated his view, adding that women should avoid joining support networks, which are like "victim's units", and get ahead by being more willing to raise their hands for line jobs and tough, risky assignments. He was accused of making the assumption that women are not as ambitious as men for the top jobs. An assortment of senior women executives waded in to talk about their own experiences of overcoming stereotype and unconscious bias to make it to the top of some of the largest American corporations.

The Catalyst report, however, provides quantitative evidence that even when women are as ambitious as men for the top jobs, they still lose out in career advancement and compensation. For example, when considering only men and women who aspired to become chief executives and senior executives, and only considering childless men and women, the research revealed glaring discrepancies:

- women had lower starting salaries in their first post-MBA job than men (even after taking account of number of years of prior experience, time since MBA, first post-MBA job level, global region and industry);
- regardless of differences in women's and men's starting salary, men experienced higher salary growth post-MBA;
- men were more likely to take a first assignment at a higher rank with greater levels of responsibilities than women, from first-level manager to chief executive/senior manager;
- men outpaced women most when they both started at the bottom of the company; men moved up the career ladder faster even if they had the same number of years' experience and received their MBA in the first year.

McKinsey's research in both the United States and Europe highlights how unconscious bias in selection and promotion decisions can unintentionally prevent women from gaining vital career experiences, especially early on in their careers. This causes them to be excluded from talent pools for senior roles. Emily Lawson explains:

> A lot of decisions are made that rule women out of [senior] roles because of assumptions about what they would and would not do. For example, "we cannot offer her that job now because she has a family and she is not going to want to work internationally", or situations where a company does not give a woman the most demanding clients because it assumes there are men there who will not interact well with her.
>
> Lots of these assumptions may be well-intentioned but they are weeding women out of the talent pool without proper discussion.

Women themselves sometimes step to the side, and McKinsey points to a lack of confidence in women and also the problem of internal politics. In a 2012 study, "Unlocking the full potential of women at work", the women who said they did not aspire to senior executive posts cited politics as the main reason. McKinsey advised that more women would go the full distance if executive committees were more attractive, displaying greater "openness, honesty, authenticity and teamwork".

Based on the McKinsey research, Lawson comments more positively:

> *The companies that are really pushing the boat out ... have firstly promotion targets and secondly unconscious bias training, which forces men and women to uncover what assumptions are informing their decisions about the world around them and the kind of jobs they are recruiting for.*

Unlike employees from generation Y, women are often reluctant to voice their ambitions and less likely to apply for promotion or opt for stretching assignments. Maggie Wilderotter, chairman and chief executive of Frontier Communications, an American telephone company, says that women tend to wait to get noticed.

> *For a lot of women, they think the myth is true, that if they do a good job and work hard, they'll get recognised. That's not the case.*

Lawson comments:

> *We run training sessions for high-ranking women in the UK. One of the issues raised is that if you don't ask, you don't get. This does not just relate to money, it also relates to promotions and increased responsibilities.*

Smaller companies may be better placed to compete for both disenchanted women and impatient young high-flyers. Rain Newton-Smith, an economist who has worked for the Bank of England and the IMF and is currently head of emerging markets at Oxford Economics, comments:

In a smaller company, you have to forge your own career a bit more than in a larger institution like the Bank of England. There are fewer places to hide behind. It was undoubtedly a risky move for me to go to Oxford Economics but it certainly worked out.

From her perspective as a boss who manages a small team of young, highly skilled economists, she says:

The advantage of a small company is that when you see a very bright employee, you can make sure you recognise their ability quickly, give them the kind of work they want, and promote them quickly. Bigger companies have to worry about hierarchies and procedures, regulations and precedents and that gets in the way.

Money and challenging work

In the 2009 Ashridge/ILM study, 33% of UK graduate respondents placed challenging or interesting work in the top three most important factors in their working life. Next in importance was a high salary (32%) and career advancement (24%).

In the 2008 Robert Half/Yahoo! Hotjobs survey of American workers from generation Y, the three most important job considerations were:

- salary;
- benefits;
- opportunities for career growth/advancement.

The Saudi-based Gulf International Bank (GIB) is building a new retail bank in the Middle East aimed at the emerging middle class in the region, and is working hard to attract high-flying graduates. The bank focuses on offering competitive salaries and the opportunity to have a fast-moving career; the new retail business is effectively a start-up venture in an otherwise staid banking sector.

The GIB's goal is to slot its graduate employees into the right roles and vacancies as they become available in the new business. Its graduate development programme prepares graduates for specific jobs in the organisation. The priority is to make sure that graduates do not finish the programme and find themselves in limbo, waiting to be slotted into a position as the retail business gets up and running.

The bank holds careers fairs in places such as American universities, targeting graduates with international experience from Saudi Arabia and other Gulf Co-operation Council countries. There is fierce competition for these graduates, not only from Middle Eastern businesses but also from Western firms that want to gain a foothold in the region.

The GIB realised that it would quickly lose graduate employees if there was nowhere for them to go in the organisation once they completed their graduate development programme. As Cornel Fourie, the bank's former chief human resources officer, explains:

> We know for 2013 what our vacancies are going to be in terms of our growth strategy. We recruit our graduates to fill those vacancies and a big percentage of the training of the talent at the very young stage is directly linked to the skills they require for the vacancy they will fill. We recruit 40 graduates a year and each one of these graduates will fill a vacancy after a year on the programme.

Fourie says that the bank retains young talent "with difficulty", and this is likely to get harder as some nearby countries, notably Dubai, scale up their recruitment efforts. Offering competitive salaries is important, but the lure of challenge and opportunity is even more so. Fourie comments:

> In my experience, I find that talented people want opportunity and the way we sometimes create opportunity is not upwards but sideways. It might be that we move someone in retail over to wholesale banking for three to six months. We rotate our staff and we also give them the opportunity to stretch. We say "over and above what you are doing at the moment, I would like you to work on a stretch project which is outside your comfort zone". A lot of our talented people thrive on these opportunities.

Both Apple and Google set great store on using exciting work assignments to attract and keep the brightest graduates.

Liane Hornsey, vice-president of people operations at Google, says:

We attract millions – and I mean millions – of applicants to Google each year. And the reason we attract millions of people to Google is because, first and foremost, everybody knows that it is a damn cool place to work. Second, because you could be working on tomorrow's biggest problem – infrastructure in Sub-Saharan Africa, robotic cars, GoogleGlass. Okay? We have very, very innovative products that attract the brightest and best.

For Apple, it is a straightforward matter of offering the best financial incentives and work opportunities. In his analysis of Apple's approach to talent management, John Sullivan, professor of management at San Francisco State University, says: "At Apple, the primary long-term attraction and retention factors are stock growth and exciting work."

The company promises "corporate jobs, without the corporate part", meaning an avoidance of endless meetings, routine tasks, bureaucracy and hierarchy. Stock ownership is the most important form of financial motivator. Most employees receive periodic stock grants to reward their contribution. Individual rewards are based on performance and consist of stock grants and cash bonuses of up to 30% of base salary.

Compared with Google, Facebook and Microsoft, Apple's benefits are "spartan", as Sullivan explains:

Because of the importance of these two factors, the message on benefits is clear. If you are doing the best work of your life and having a major impact on the world, do you really need sushi in the cafeteria?

Many employees, not just people from generation Y, want challenging work, as is evidenced time and again in engagement studies. However, Emily Lawson makes the observation that this is an especially effective means of retaining women after a career break:

One of the things we know is that if we can get women into roles where they perceive themselves to be making a difference before they have children, they are twice as likely to come back to work afterwards. If they are in a relatively low level job where they feel anyone can do it, they are less likely to come back.

Opportunity to innovate

Organisations with experience of employees from generation Y believe that they particularly thrive when given opportunities to innovate. Khurshed Dehnugara, a partner at Relume, a UK research and advisory firm, says that this can be difficult for older managers to handle. Formerly commercial director at GlaxoSmithKline for ten years, Dehnugara has written about "the challenger spirit" needed in organisations. He comments:

> *On the one hand, the next generation is desperately excited by some of the new trends [such as social media and the digital industries], while we are scared. The difficulty is that they come expecting this exciting, often anxiety-provoking career – they are up for it, they are up for quite a bit of disturbance and quite a high degree of personal risk and commitment.*
>
> *Then they come into environments where the company will only move when it is absolutely certain about a trend. That is really depressing for them. This next generation loses heart, they lose energy. They either leave or the seat is warm but the brain is not really there. I think they are more ready than we imagine they are and we are not providing an environment in which they can thrive.*

Many entrepreneurial women have been unwilling to wait for more conducive conditions and have left to start their own business. The implications for talent management are explored in Chapter 6, but it is worth looking at the reasons these women leave.

A 2001 study by Korn/Ferry International, one of the world's largest executive firms, provided some valuable insights into the motivation of women who had quit senior positions in corporations to start their own business. The reasons for leaving were positive and opportunistic – but they serve as an indictment of their previous employers. Based on the responses of 425 women (of whom 30% were former directors, 27% were vice-presidents and 9% had top roles such as chief executive and president), the top three reasons for leaving their corporations were the opportunity to:

- take risks and test personal ideas;
- create wealth;
- have an impact on strategic issues.

The Korn/Ferry study noted that large companies were losing the "war for talent" in the case of innovative and entrepreneurial women. The conclusion, made over a decade ago, still rings true today:

> This top talent looks to the small business setting for their next career move. Unlike previous decades, today's businesswomen do not consider the large corporate environment as the ideal place to pursue their dreams of innovation and creativity. In fact, many of them are taking the skills they learned in the corporate setting and applying them to new positions in the small business world, either as owners or non-owners ... The women we studied have strong desires to pioneer new innovations – generating ideas, developing ideas and learning from their impact. Corporations would be well advised to consider the role of women ... offering them more control over the strategic process and reducing constraints on creativity if they hope to retain [their] talent.

Work–life balance

The 2009 Ashridge/ILM study suggests that although generation Y graduates are ambitious, they want a good work–life balance, ranking this as fifth most important in their working life. They tend not to take work home with them but they expect to be able to undertake personal tasks while at work.

In the 2008 Robert Half/Yahoo! Hotjobs survey, having work–life balance was ranked the third most important aspect of generation Y's work environment. Some 73% of respondents said they were concerned about balancing work and personal obligations.

This shift in motivation is apparent among young MBA students, according to both London Business School and IMD. Fiona Sandford, executive director, global business and careers at London Business School, comments that today's students are "more thoughtful" about what they want from their careers: "What we are finally seeing is what everybody in 2008 predicted – which is a change in student ambitions." She says that MBA students are no longer automatically applying for positions in big global banks or the top-tier strategy consultancies:

> We are seeing students being a little more thoughtful. Very often it is about achieving the right work–life balance. If you are working for one of those wonderful consultancies, you are not going to have much of a life. You are going to be working excessively hard for quite a long period. And for some graduates, this is just not right.

Claire Lecoq of IMD has noticed the same trend among MBA students (who tend to be slightly older than MBA students generally and in middle-management roles):

> They are definitely looking for something different. There is a much stronger desire for life balance. Even five years ago, you would have had people opting for careers in finance or consulting, but now MBA students are definitely looking at life balance and this is high on their list when they are approaching a company [to explore job opportunities].

She believes that some of the emphasis on work–life balance among younger managers is because of their reluctance to give their employer the same degree of loyalty as their parents did. Perhaps because of the economic crisis, they are less drawn to a traditional career in a big organisation:

> These shifts started about five to seven years ago, but now it is a deep trend. This generation is not going to sacrifice everything for their career as their parents did. They are more balanced – they want a career but their life and family is important. We are seeing a much bigger desire among our students to being their own boss, contributing to society and living a better life.

Sandra Schwarzer of INSEAD agrees:

> This generation for me is the generation that has seen their parents and grandparents lose their jobs – so their loyalties have shifted. They are much more loyal to themselves than to any one organisation. I don't think it is selfishness, it is a matter of trust …

*Whether it is due to the economic downturn, I also think a lot of
them have been faced with setbacks. They have developed a certain
resilience. They know they cannot rely on an organisation, they
have to rely on themselves.*

McKinsey's 2012 study found that women slow their careers or
shift roles, especially from line management to staff roles, to obtain
more predictable working hours and to reduce the need to travel
for work. This often occurs at a critical time when the talent system
requires them to be mobile, gain international exposure and take
tough developmental assignments.

Women can take themselves out of the "talent game", but
high-flying women can take the more drastic step of leaving the
organisation altogether.

Lisa Calvert, senior vice-president, human resources and facilities,
at Getty Images, an American company that creates and distributes
images, footage and music online, stresses that large corporations
need to remember that talented women always have "the freedom
to choose". She says:

*My perspective on women and unlocking leadership positions
is simply that women have choice. I'm very fortunate. I work for
a very creative company. It's young, it is 17 years old. It is 50%
women. I have worked for much larger corporations but I chose to
leave. I did not feel I was getting the support that I needed to move
myself along in my career. I knew "aspirationally" where I wanted
to go as a woman.*

*I had to make a hard choice. I had to make a choice about my
family and my children, work–life balance and all of these things.
I chose to go to an organisation that supported all of those things
for me ... It sometimes takes that kind of initiative by women to
have the people who are making the decisions to wake up and ask
"is this a problem for us?" and "do we really care?".*

Freedom and autonomy at work

The graduates in the Ashridge/ILM study valued a high degree of
freedom and autonomy, both in how their work was organised and

how they were treated by their boss. They did not want their managers "watching over their shoulder" or "behaving in a controlling and micro-managing way".

Asked about what behaviour was most important in their line manager, graduate respondents ranked as their top three:

- respects and values the graduate;
- trusts the graduate to get on with things;
- communicates well to the graduate.

The two lowest-ranked behaviours were setting clear objectives and providing regular feedback about the graduate's performance. However, managers in the study said that regular feedback about performance and setting clear objectives were the most important management behaviours for them to display. The report points to a "significant disconnect between graduates and managers" in how they view their relationship. For example:

- Graduates define their ideal manager as a coach or mentor (56%) or friend (21%), rather than someone who directs (8%) or examines and audits (2%).
- Some 19% of graduates view their manager as someone who directs and allocates work, while only 9% of managers believe they act this way.
- Just 26% of graduates think their manager acts as a coach or mentor, while 75% of managers believe they fulfil this role.

Fiona Sandford of London Business School says that the desire for autonomy is an equally powerful motivator for young undergraduates and MBA students:

> We see it with our undergraduate management students who are 22 to 23, but we are seeing it increasingly with our MBA students. And the magic word is "autonomy" – that's what people look for and that's the word that crops up time and again.

Do these two groups define autonomy in the same way? Sandford says not quite:

With classic Gen Ys, they think they can rule the world now, thank you, and would like to get on with it! More grown-up MBA students want to be valued for their intellect and their skills. They want someone to really value their toolkit and their soft skills, to trust them to manage their own work and to follow up their clients.

Clearly, the task of providing the right degree of freedom and autonomy lies with line managers – and hence they have a pivotal role to play in ensuring their rising stars remain challenged and engaged.

Becky Snow, global talent director at Mars, is aware of the importance of bosses in any talent management system:

There is loads of research around the fact that people leave bosses, not companies, and I really wonder just how much individual leaders will come to the fore, especially as companies do so much work to position themselves as forces for good.

Middle-manager engagement

Middle managers play a crucially important role in engaging rising talent. A number of employees interviewed for this book mentioned how middle managers can open doors for younger talent by allowing them to spread their wings. However, middle managers can also block talent if they so choose.

The Gulf International Bank's move into retail banking has led to it targeting its recruitment at smart young graduates, but this has sometimes caused tensions with more conservative middle managers who joined the bank before this shift in strategy. As Cornel Fourie explains:

Sometimes our existing middle managers act like a layer of mud and cause our talented people to leave. This is because some middle managers are intimidated by talented people, especially by their knowledge, and manage them at arm's length. They themselves don't want to go anywhere and they won't move – this is often a turn off for a lot of talented people.

The GIB has tackled this issue by creating talent management committees to make sure that promotion decisions are taken collectively rather than by a few individuals. The bank is also moving to a coaching-based culture to make sure that staff are developed and stretched.

PepsiCo takes prompt action when it sees managers standing in the way of ambitious younger managers. Richard Evans, president, PepsiCo UK, Ireland & South Africa, asserts:

> If anyone is seen to be blocking someone, they are called aside by senior managers and "named and shamed". This is because if you get in the way of promising staff, why are they going to stay with us? All that happens is that they see the block and they leave because there is always a market for talent elsewhere.

Google also values internal coaching as a way of supporting staff and empowering them to take risks and even fail. For Google's innovative environment to work, Liane Hornsey explains:

> We allow people the freedom to fail and the freedom to keep their job if they fail because they had the guts to take the initiative.

Internal coaches play a vital role in supporting people to work in this way. Hornsey comments:

> In an environment where there is a lot of trust, I don't have an issue where people might be frightened to be open to internal coaches. That really helps.

Coaching is often cross-functional, and Hornsey believes that this helps break down functional barriers between engineers and sales people and also helps develop leaders:

> One way of developing great managers and leaders is to get them to become great coaches. They learn listening skills, they learn not to be impulsive. They learn not to give all the answers every time.

Implications: personalised career management

The previous chapter outlined how some international companies are seeking to build talent by giving employees the width and depth of experience, especially in terms of international assignments, that will make them valuable to the business in the long term. Unfortunately for them, it seems that many talented people are not interested in staying with the firm long term.

Jon Ingham, a human resources and organisation development consultant, spells out the challenge to organisations but also provides a positive note:

> *Organisations are going to have to adjust or they won't be able to recruit, retain and engage [generation Y] individuals. But organisations are going to have to appeal to older workers who have the same requirements.*
>
> *The good thing is that the changes organisations are going to have to make to appeal to Gen Y are positive things anyway – being more collaborative, having a purpose, focusing on individual employees. It is all the things HR people in particular should be crying out in their organisations to create. This is a wonderful enabler for all of us.*

If high-potential, high-performing employees are not lost to the business, through being poached by a rival or through self-employment, employers have to find ways of creating a compelling "employee value proposition", which, in plain English, means supplying them with the right set of inducements to stay.

This means brokering a deal with the talented individual, such that the company can offer career opportunities that both satisfy the needs of the business and cater for personal circumstances and the set of values, goals and needs driving a talented individual. In a nutshell, the challenge is no longer to "manage" talent – it is to keep talented individuals fulfilled.

Career planning therefore needs to be highly tailored and personal for anyone whose contribution is crucial in the longer term. If the needs of people from generation Y, women and increasingly other groups of talented employees are catered for, personalised career management needs to incorporate the following good practices.

Open and honest career discussions

The purpose is to ensure clarity and alignment with what the individual wants and expects from the organisation in terms of career goals, and how this can fit with business goals. These discussions are a particular means of managing the expectations of impatient or overambitious employees from generation Y. They are also an opportunity for talented individuals to voice any anxieties and to look at any personal issues that might prevent them from taking advantages of career or development opportunities.

Google works actively to help graduates from generation Y to start to think differently about their careers and to have more realistic expectations. Their fixation with a vertical career is quickly challenged, as Liane Hornsey recounts:

> These graduates come out of school and expect the world and expect you to give them a career path tomorrow. They are kids that expect it to be all planned out for them over the next eight years and then they are going to be chief executive. Well hey, let's get real at this point. But because we do have kids of this generation, we present our programmes in a way that actually looks like it is progression ... we do this so they can feel a sense of movement ... We try to wean them off the career path idea – actually my view is that it is a jungle gym, not a career ladder.

The Boston Consulting Group says that these types of discussions are like "a very interactive, high touch kind of agreement", and that it is seeing more corporate clients moving towards this. This is especially true in fast-growing markets where talented employees expect to move rapidly and will leave if they think there are better opportunities elsewhere. Jean-Michel Caye, a BCG fellow who heads the HR/people advantages and talent topics for the group globally, observes:

> The more you are in a competitive marketplace as a company, the more competitive people are individually and the more people's career management is individual too.

Personalised career opportunities

The purpose is to make plans that take into account the different career goals of talented individuals and to make sure that the organisation provides individuals with the right job experiences at the right time. In some cases, the organisation may be able to outline a specific career path; but in many cases, it may be a set of abilities that individuals need to acquire at that stage of their career.

Some individuals may want to progress rapidly to a senior role and the emphasis is on providing an accelerated career path. Others might want a senior role that lets them remain in the region and some will be looking for international or global roles. Other talented individuals might be happy to deepen their specialist skills and welcome opportunities for lateral moves rather than progressing upwards.

Sandra Schwarzer of INSEAD makes two points about personalised career planning. On the one hand, she says that a close partnership between the individual and HR is key to help manage expectations:

> There is often hunger on the part of the talent to be recognised and it is difficult to manage that because in a corporate setting, you cannot advance people quickly. Communication is key.

On the other hand, talented individuals also need to recognise that it is not always possible for their companies to give them a neat series of career steps, given the complexity and uncertainty of the business environment.

Companies may be able to identify the skills and experiences that are critical at each career stage, but they may not be able to specify specific positions or roles. It is the individual's responsibility to be self-aware and to think about what they want from their career. Schwarzer comments:

> We have a couple of graphs that show students that there are
> 15 different ways to get to country manager because we have
> interviewed all our alumni who worked in that role. We have listed
> all the different stations that they have had in their career – and there
> is no one path. What we try to tell them is that in today's life, you

can look maybe one or two steps ahead, but you may be asked to step sideways too.

Students are encouraged to become more self-aware, says Schwarzer:

We make them aware that if they are in command of their career, they need regular time to think about what it is that they want and how do they get it, how do they maintain their learning and how do they continue to develop themselves.

The company needs to be aware of and take into account when the individual might desire (or require) extended leave, or a job closer to home with more regular hours. And career planning should identify what experience the individual will need to progress.

In the case of women, all McKinsey's research points to the importance of making sure that women genuinely get the same access as men to stretching assignments, adequate line-management experience and sponsorship from senior leaders to increase their visibility and make sure they are considered for key roles in the organisation.

Emily Lawson says planning should be as early as possible for both men and women:

Most companies don't invest in people until their late 30s and early 40s. You need to spot them much earlier. You need to get them on the right career path, learning languages and getting the right kind of experiences before they have families and children and they are stuck in one place.

Frequent career reviews

The goal is to make sure that the career of talented individuals is progressing as expected and is not being blocked by unnecessary barriers. These reviews should also make sure that talented people are not trapped in pockets of the organisation or that careers are not derailed at certain career stages, for example the transition from a regional to an international role. Line managers play an important role in making sure that their talented people are thriving, but in many companies a committee of senior managers and the HR/talent management function also hold regular reviews.

At Randstad, for example, senior managers and HR staff devote considerable time to talent reviews. Many parts of the organisation are involved in discussions to help build a shared picture of how talented people are deployed in the business. The process involves in-depth reviews by a board member together with the leadership team and HR staff, and line managers assess individuals at every stage of their career. Marielle de Macker, HR managing director, says:

> A formal talent review takes place once a year, but the responsibility for spotting talent identification is certainly not limited to HR professionals only. Each and every leader in our company is always looking out for, monitoring, observing and developing talent, each and every day.

Career trellises instead of career paths

A career trellis offers multiple career options so that employees can alter the speed and direction of their career, whereas a career ladder focuses on vertical career moves. Career trellises work well for those who want to broaden their experience and for organisations where there are limited opportunities for promotion. They offer, for example, temporary assignments, lateral moves and stretching projects, which may be in unfamiliar markets or a role in a short-term joint-venture project.

Boston Consulting Group believes that career trellises give employees better opportunities for career advancement. Jean-Michel Caye explains:

> There are two ideas there. The first is that organisations have become flatter and people are more energised and free to use their discretion. So there are fewer ladders to climb. Second, competence development has become more demanding. In many cases, you will have to get a variety of experiences to develop the right level of competence. So you sometimes move laterally and sometimes move diagonally.

Google sets great store on rotating its people between posts to challenge them and keep them engaged. Following talent mapping and reviews, it develops people through a global rotation programme, where people are circulated around different regional offices. Liane Hornsey says:

> We do a lot of work to get people to sit down and think, "actually, what do I want to do?" And of course, in order to do that you have to give them a sense of what is available.

However, this method depends on employing what the company calls "general athletes", as Hornsey explains:

> I think this is important because if you select people who have general capabilities and you are willing to rotate them as we are, you can keep them learning, keep them happy, and give them broader experience.

By the time a person gets to a senior level, they have plenty of cross-functional experience and are "more rounded before they join the executive". Moving people in this way is disruptive to the business, but Hornsey says it is worth it.

Apple

Apple's approach to career management is clear: the company insists that its employees take complete control of their career management. The concept of having employees "own their career" has been in place for some years. Apple believes that if it constructs a career path for its staff, employees will develop a "sense of entitlement" and assume that they have a right to continuous promotion.

According to John Sullivan of San Francisco State University, Apple believes that career paths weaken employee self-reliance and indirectly make cross-departmental collaboration and learning less likely. In the absence of a conventional career path, he explains:

> Employees actively seek out information about jobs in other functions and business units. In a company where creativity and innovation are king, you

don't want anything reducing your employee's curiosity and the cross-pollination between diverse functions and units.

Apple rarely moves employees automatically up to the next functional job, because it believes this may also severely narrow the range of internal movement within the organisation. It thinks that less mobility will also reduce the level of diverse thinking in some groups.

Flexible working arrangements

Any company that is serious about diversity will enable employees with family commitments to work shorter hours or part time, job share, or take extended leave as part of maternity or paternity arrangements. It is not just parents who want more flexibility but also people from generation Y and older workers.

McKinsey's research suggests that among women few managers or senior staff currently enjoy flexible working arrangements. American research in 2012, which involved interviews with 350 executives in 60 companies and a survey of 4,000 employees in 14 of those companies, noted that half of the women surveyed were both the primary breadwinner and principal provider of care at home. The majority of men who were the primary breadwinner were not the principal provider of care at home. The report said:

In this context, the fact that only 3% of managers (men and women) worked part time and that less than 1% of more senior executives work part time makes balance tough for mothers. While some companies have created flexible work arrangements, part-time plans remain elusive.

This is as pertinent in a 2012 study of 235 European companies, *Making the Breakthrough*, which suggested that "working less than full-time is still seen as a risky career move that can deter women from making it". McKinsey recommends the following:

Flexible working is likely to catch on fully only when it ceases to be regarded as the preserve of women with dependents. In one company, when men began to take advantage of the flexible work programme, a tipping point was reached at which flexible working became commonplace, and over the course of five years, the senior management team was transformed.

Role models help. Senior managers, both men and women, who discuss their flexible working patterns can help demonstrate that it is possible to be successful and committed to the business and still work flexibly.

Tailored learning and development opportunities

The opportunity to develop further skills and learning is an essential means to make sure that talented employees feel engaged in their work and that their potential is recognised. Such development must be continuous if valued employees are to remain motivated at times when the opportunity for promotion or new responsibilities is minimal.

Stretching assignments play a critical role in helping people learn on the job. In the case of individuals who are unable to work abroad, companies are using shorter international stretching projects that focus on personal development.

Chartered Institute of Personnel and Development research into the experience of belonging to a talent pool revealed that respondents to the survey rated the opportunity to develop new skills as the second most important benefit of being talent managed. They valued unstructured on-the-job learning more than formal programmes. The three most highly rated developmental opportunities were coaching (50%), mentoring (38%) and high-quality feedback (38%). The CIPD notes:

> *Self-awareness is a commonly perceived benefit from coaching and mentoring. The value placed on these less structured, more individually based development activities is consistent across organisations, sectors and grades of individuals.*

Part of Santander UK's talent strategy revolves around providing high-potential employees with many developmental opportunities early in their careers. These include apprenticeships, internships, internal courses to gain formal banking qualifications, job rotation, volunteering schemes and leadership development programmes. Caroline Curtis, head of talent, succession and leadership development, explains the rationale:

> We ensure individual development plans are put in place, for example, we have a number of people working on internal projects where they have an opportunity to experience different parts of the operation – across a number of different geographies. This chance to develop real skills in a real life environment is hugely beneficial. I am also a huge fan of mentoring, coaching and buddying – with all parties gaining from the relationship.

Michael Stanford, executive director of IMD, says the business school is seeing more examples of companies that are taking a strategic view of both forms of development and successfully blending the two in their talent management work. He comments:

> Many organisations recognise that while development work designed for the organisation might be an excellent source of organisation capability-building, it might not satisfy the desire of each individual to create and explore his or her own world of curiosity and learning without a specific organisational objective in mind.

Stanford says that the task of creating an integrated learning and development portfolio that includes "highly personalised development work" is difficult:

> It is not always obvious how an organisation's strategy can be translated into organisational capabilities and finally distilled to individual development plans ... the task of creating such individualised development is time consuming and sometimes difficult.

IMD's "hybrid programmes" include a mix of company-specific programme work aimed at collective capability-building, individual coaching and mentoring, individual action-learning projects and relevant open programmes which emphasise how to make sure that individual learning is successfully applied in the workplace.

Coaching, mentoring and sponsorship

Coaching, mentoring and sponsoring have proved to be effective in helping talented people to develop and feel valued, and they provide a good way for senior managers to take an active role in nurturing gifted people.

Coaching

The theory is simple, but the 2009 Ashridge/ILM research into people from generation Y shows that the practice of coaching is anything but simple. In essence, a coach focuses on helping more junior, less-experienced individuals improve their performance and results. The aim is to help them broaden their skill base, knowledge and understanding of their role rather than solely providing feedback and moral support.

The people interviewed wanted their line managers to act as coaches, but the majority felt they failed to do so. Conversely, managers believed that they performed this role.

The problem lies in the failure to deliver "authentic coaching", according to Ashridge. Managers need to "adjust the way they think about and practice management", appreciate the differences between mentoring and coaching, and improve their coaching skills. And their organisations need to work harder to create a culture of coaching.

Mentoring

Mentors provide career advice, feedback on how to improve and also act as role models. The focus is less on current performance and more on an individual's potential and aspirations. There is a wealth of evidence to show that mentoring especially helps talented people to advance at senior managerial levels.

For example, Catalyst looked at the benefits of mentoring via an online survey conducted in 2008 of more than 4,000 MBA alumni who graduated between 1996 and 2007 from top schools in Asia, Canada, Europe and the United States. The resulting report published in 2010 noted:

> We found that mentors have an impact on high potentials' career advancement from day one and continue to have an impact as

careers progress – although men reaped greater salary increases from mentoring than women.

Mentoring – especially from senior-level mentors – enabled both men and women to advance up the corporate ladder. The analysis revealed that high-potential people with current mentoring relationships received significantly more promotions. However, what really counted was the mentor's level of seniority. For example:

- those with mentors at the CEO or senior management level received more promotions;
- women who had mentors at the top got promoted at the same rate as men who had such mentors – but more men than women had a mentor at the CEO or senior management level (62% of men versus 52% of women).

Overall, mentoring was critical for the progression of men and women to the highest level, but it was not sufficient to help women catch up with men in terms of salary. The findings of the research prompted Catalyst to introduce the concept of sponsorship as a way of accelerating the careers of women.

Sponsorship

Nancy Carter and Christine Silva of Catalyst define sponsorship as:

The active support by an individual placed in the organisation with sufficient influence on the decision-making process and who is advocating for, protecting and fighting for the career advancement of the individual.

A 2012 Catalyst report explored the concept of sponsorship further by interviewing 93 male and female executives. The findings suggest that sponsorship can have a powerful influence on people's route to top management. It is especially beneficial to women, providing them with access to the most influential networks within their organisation.

The report cites the example of Deutsche Bank, which created a one-year sponsorship programme in 2009 for high-performing women from its business units globally. The aim is to help these women reach executive leadership positions by pairing them with members of the bank's group executive committee from a different business line.

Sponsors can also help women to be more confident in their careers. Research in 2012 by the UK-based Centre for Talent Innovation demonstrates that women in the UK with sponsors are 52% more likely to be satisfied with their rate of advancement than those without. With a sponsor's backing, they are 25% more likely to ask for a pay rise and 58% less likely to consider quitting their job within one year.

Sponsors have a significant influence on the careers of mothers. Unsponsored working mothers are more than twice as likely as their sponsored peers – 14% compared with 6% – to plan on leaving their organisation within a year.

PepsiCo

PepsiCo, a multinational food and beverage corporation, has rethought its approach to career planning in response to talent shortages and because it needs to make sure that the next generation of senior managers have a variety of assignments across the company's global business. This involves taking a much longer perspective of individuals' careers and pinpointing when they are most likely to be mobile and when family commitments are likely to ground them in their home country.

Individuals who are earmarked for senior management posts have an in-depth interview, where they are asked what might influence their desire and ability to take up international assignments. This might include their spouse's career plans, considerations about their children's education or whether they are the primary carers for ageing parents.

Richard Evans, president, PepsiCo UK, Ireland and South Africa, says these "intelligent profiles" have resulted in a different type of conversation between the company and its high-potential employees:

You have to change the style of the conversation you have with people. We have gone from a very formal conversation to a more informal 'can do' career conversation, where you build a level of trust with the people you are talking to.

Conclusion

Increasing numbers of employees, not just women and people from generation Y, are taking an individualistic approach to their careers and may not be willing to sacrifice everything to get to the top. Talented individuals appear much less loyal to their organisations. They are strongly committed to developing their own talent and pursuing their personal goals before those of the organisation.

Organisations need to take on board this new reality and offer the right development opportunities and work experiences – otherwise talented people will leave.

Flexible career planning can help satisfy talented people, but it may not be sufficient to gain their trust and loyalty. Despite the best processes, some talented individuals continue to enter companies, learn what they can and then move on, throwing succession plans into disarray.

The next chapter looks at how companies can connect with their talented people in terms of shared purpose and values and whether it is possible to build a culture where talented people become willing and equal partners in the talent game.

5 Taking a culture-led approach

Something that I do think it is worth emphasising, is corporate responsibility. Time and time again, it has been shown that Gen Y really do care to work for an organisation that really is having a positive impact on the world and society or on a community.

Lucian Tarnowski, founder and chief executive,
BraveNewTalent.com

In Chapter 2, Joydeep Bose, Olam International's president and global head of human resources, described how the company is attempting to bond the disparate businesses and assets it owns through a common culture linked by such attributes as ambition, entrepreneurship and empowerment.

Olam is not the only company exploring this approach. With a new generation of workers who do not see long-term employment and systematic promotion and development over decades as an incentive to stay with a company, and emerging talent who are becoming picky about who they work for (see Chapter 4), stating publicly what a company stands for and developing a culture that shows how its values are "lived" in practice are being seen increasingly as a way to "bond" talented people.

AT&T, a multinational telecommunications corporation, starts communicating its values and culture well before any formal recruitment process. It has created a "talent network", which has proved highly successful in "connecting and reaching out" to a large pool of job seekers, according to Carrie Corbin, associate director of talent acquisition. The company must reach 20m job seekers per year and "seriously consider" 250,000–1,000,000 of these to meet its hiring needs.

Job seekers join the talent network and are kept informed of potential job opportunities through, for example, a careers website, a talent network Facebook application, a mobile careers website. They also receive periodic information about jobs and a monthly newsletter. When looking for candidates to fill new vacancies, the company's recruitment staff go to the talent network first.

When AT&T surveyed 95,000 talent-network members, it was surprised to learn that they placed most value on receiving news of the company and that they felt "more connected" as a result. According to TMP Worldwide, a recruitment advertising agency, by mid-2010 the talent network had 562,178 members, with membership growing by an average of 18% each month; the unsubscribe rate was less than a 1%.

Those interviewed for this book confirm the importance of some form of connection with a company's values and culture. For example, Sanjar Ibragimov, an IMD MBA graduate, says that one of the deciding factors in choosing to work for DuPont was his identification with its values:

> I saw from my experience of being an adviser to many companies that there is often huge discrepancy between the aims and the way they are executed. When I came to DuPont, I realised that their core values were really in the DNA of the company: safety, environmental stewardship, care for people.
>
> I was really touched by this. I have been working here for six months already and I really see that they mean what they say. I find myself in the right place and I am happy that these core values are my core values as well. It was something deeply instilled in me from my very early years.

Ian Pearman, chief executive of Abbott Mead Vickers, joined and stayed with the company for similar reasons:

> I was very lucky to find a company which dovetailed with my personal values set. At the time I didn't think about it in those terms – it is an inevitable post-rationalisation of what happened – but there was a gut feel which was an intuitive part of that decision. As an aspiring graduate coming through the Milk Round, you put yourself

*out there, you fill in 20 forms and see what comes back. I was very
lucky in that one of the agencies that I wanted to work at was this
one and I was lucky to be accepted.*

*Why? Well there were 2–3 things. Firstly, they had policies
that I found very unusual for advertising. For example, we have
a principled stand against children's toys advertising. We don't
advertise anything overtly to children because of the "pester power"
effect. This is founded on a belief that you should only advertise
to people who have the full mental capability to make informed
decisions.*

*At the time it was set up, the company also refused to take
smoking advertising. This was 30 years ago when it was very
tempting to take tobacco accounts. Principles cost you money and
I found it really interesting and distinctive that the company stood
by its principles. I thought the company had a philosophy that was
coherent and compelling.*

*And this is even more important now than it was then. In
the past ten years, the authenticity of branding in the consumer
products arena has been so pronounced that today's young aspirant
graduates are trained in their role as consumers to look for brands
and companies that have some kind of mission and vision which is
conducive to social good.*

Many talent management experts agree that more aspiring high-
flyers think in this way. James Cullens, group human resources
director at Hays, observes:

*I guess there is also a very strong call from candidates in terms of
"what is the purpose of the organisation that I am going to work
for". They take the attitude: "I'm going to be much more selective
about what I am going to do. I may actually fiddle around with my
own business doing my own thing until I find the right opportunity.*

*"So no longer am I going to do the traditional round of Mars and
Unilever and build my CV in the way my father would have done.
Actually I am going to take a very different and more piecemeal
approach to planning the experiences that I want – because I know
that I am going to be working until I am 87 – so I might as well do
stuff that I enjoy."*

That's the difference and so people are looking at their careers in a different way from the way we would have done, certainly when we started off.

Emily Lawson of McKinsey agrees:

The management of culture in organisations has become more important. We are adopting a very different approach to setting and maintaining norms, evaluating people against them and establishing the fabric of the organisation, both in the wake of the financial crisis and also in the wake of the need to manage companies in a more connected world.

Culture-led approaches in practice

A good example of a company that has taken a culture-led approach in its recruitment and retention of talented staff is Naukri.com, an Indian online recruitment company founded in 1997. At that time there were only 14,000 internet users in India; 12 years and an estimated 50m internet users later, it has come a long way. After an initial public offering and expansion into other related businesses under the umbrella of its Info Edge parent company, by 2009 Naukri had become India's leading online recruitment company.

From the start, Naukri encouraged an organisational culture that valued energy, enthusiasm, youth and experimentation. This contrasted with the more hierarchical structure at many Indian companies and helped it position itself as the hot dotcom business in India for young, bright talent.

One of Naukri's attractions had been its employee stock option plan (ESOP). But when the Indian stockmarket plunged following the onset of the global financial crisis in late 2008, this lost its appeal as a hiring and retention tool. Senior executives feared that several employees would be tempted by job offers from other technology companies.

Personnel decisions had always been crucial to Naukri's growth and development. Now the challenge was to adjust the hiring and retention strategy and keep employees motivated. It decided to focus more on providing a compelling rationale for working at Naukri rather than anywhere else.

Knowing that the falling share price had made the ESOP less attractive, Sanjeev Bikhchandani, the company's co-founder and chief executive, and Hitesh Oberoi, who went on to become the chief operating officer, took two quick steps to address employees' financial concerns. First, instead of offering new ESOPs at the market price, which had been standard policy, they offered them at a lower price, so employees could see value in them. Second, they introduced monthly financial incentives for the sales team, replacing the previous quarterly scheme that was similar to those at many other Indian companies.

Crucially, however, Bikhchandani and Oberoi also emphasised the company's culture, portraying Naukri as a business that represented the new, young, vibrant India, offering a fun work environment and the chance to grow within the organisation. They pointed out that working for a large American tech company might seem tempting, but employees would probably have to wait much longer to get to a senior level with the ability to make things happen. At Naukri, by contrast, anyone in the marketing or technical department with an idea for improving the company website could get this implemented immediately and see the impact of their creativity.

As a result, most of the members of the top team from the founding stage have stayed with the company. Personnel turnover is low compared with other companies in the online recruitment sector, and in particular when compared with India's technology and business-process outsourcing (BPO) industries. Furthermore, several senior managers who left Naukri subsequently returned.

The lessons, according to Bikhchandani and Oberoi, are that companies must have a compelling rationale at all times for people to work for them; and they should be ready to manage talent through the boom and bust cycle, especially in an emerging economy.

Trying to create a culture that is vibrant and innovative has also been a challenge for Tata Chemicals. Budaraju Sudhakar, chief human resources officer, tells the story:

Six years ago we wanted to move from being a commodity company to a speciality chemicals company. We set up an innovation centre. But everything that the innovation centre guys did was regarded as useless by the commodity people because the level of investment and return was too low.

We initially tried to encourage senior people to mentor and support young entrepreneurs and innovators who were working on new products – but it didn't work out well at all. The patience level of the senior leadership was very limited, working only on the financial timeframes they were used to.

So we brought in independent directors on the board to be the mentors of these people. That worked phenomenally well because the independent directors had a very long-term view of the organisation. They didn't have a physical stake in terms of a financial return. They were also on the boards of other companies as well. They were able to neutralise the urgency of the business heads and support long-term development of business and product lines that would change the nature of the organisation.

The most important example is the water filter we developed for use in local villages. For many years, it was delayed but the independent directors were so supportive of the whole process that it was fast-tracked.

What it has achieved is to change the whole image of Tata Chemicals. Even if the company sells 1m filters every year, it just makes $20m – a very small contribution to the $300 billion revenue we earn. But the kind of reputation it has given to the company as an innovative company and not just a commodities company has been so powerful.

The value of that is so much more powerful as a recruiting tool for talent. Initially we had difficulties attracting the right kind of talent because of our image as an old-fashioned manufacturing company. Now they want to be part of this new innovative energy, producing new products and new services. That has an immense value.

Making culture-led approaches work

The experiences of Naukri and Tata Chemicals, as well as Olam International and AT&T, point to a number of characteristics that need to be in place if a culture-led approach is to work.

Senior management endorsement

The values that underpin the culture of an organisation must be embraced – and be seen to be embraced – by the chief executive and the senior management team.

Indra Nooyi, chairman and chief executive of PepsiCo, champions this view. She has taken the lead in "bonding" the senior management team to the company by emphasising that "they are PepsiCo" and treating them as a family. She also aims to get to know the up-and-coming executives in the talent pipeline. As she explains:

> *In groups of 10–15 I take them away for two days and I do 5–6 of these sessions every year – just me and these 15 people. We have no agenda. Each of us talks about ourselves. I talk about myself. They are allowed to ask any question they want.*
>
> *We go off to some little inn, we sit together for 12–15 hours a day, put our feet up – there is no structure and nobody writes notes – and we intersperse getting to know each other personally with any question that might help about the business.*
>
> *What we are making happen in PepsiCo is getting executives to think of this as a company where you don't work for PepsiCo – you are PepsiCo. You have to represent a piece of the soul of the company.*
>
> *A company is about its people. It is not about the bricks, it is not about the plants, it is about the people. The more we can invest in these kinds of emotional exercises to create the bonds, so much the better.*

More idiosyncratically, Nooyi writes to the parents of her top executives thanking them for the "gift" of their son or daughter to PepsiCo. Inspired by the pride that her mother displayed to friends, family and neighbours when her daughter was appointed chief executive of one of the world's most successful corporations, she realised that enlisting the enthusiasm and support of senior managers' families was critical in them remaining "bonded" to the company. She even goes further and takes time out from business trips to visit the parents of her top executives who live in the country.

Nooyi concludes:

I think going forward all of us need to rewrite the book on talent management. In the past the CEO said emotion has to be divorced from work. I think the new CEO has to bring in an abundance of emotion to the job. Talent is going to be in short supply. If you don't bring in that emotion equation to work I think your talent is going to abandon you.

She seeks to engage the rest of the workforce through similarly personal means. As she explains:

Every two weeks I write to all the employees in PepsiCo: all 285,000 of them. These letters are not about making plans or making sure you sell the products. They talk about me as a CEO. I might write to them and say I am taking my daughter to school today and my daughter is in the senior year and I am heartbroken – what am I going to do after she leaves home? And I will get 2,000 responses about what to do.

Or I write to them saying all of us have ageing parents. Make sure you call your parents often enough. If you call them once a week, add that extra call. And if your parents tell you on the phone that they have lots of aches and pains, it is not because they have aches and pains. If they tell you they are fine, you will hang up quickly. If they tell you that they have aches and pains, you will spend time talking to them. I talk to my mother twice a day. Most employees told me that their parents thanked me for the letter I sent them because all of them reached out to their parents more.

I have also invited guest writers among my senior executives so that the organisation understands that real people run PepsiCo: real people with real issues. That is what we are trying to do to bond people to the company.

Integration into talent development

A corporation's commitment to the global community needs to be reflected in the way it develops its top talent.

Olam International believes that it is good business to look after the interests of its stakeholders. Its chief executive, Sunny Verghese, says:

It is the responsibility of every 21st century company to be a positive force for sustainable change in the countries and contexts in which it operates.

Top-tier business graduates, particularly those originating from or keen to work in emerging markets, are in high demand from multinational corporations keen to develop their growth-market operations. To successfully attract and retain these people, Olam tries to appeal to their need for a "higher purpose" in their work; the opportunity to make a difference while also pursuing a successful career.

Olam encourages its managers to invest in local communities to improve the livelihoods and resources of the people working for local suppliers.

A similar sense of community consciousness is encouraged by Hays, as James Cullens describes:

We are spending time trying to create an environment for community-minded people to come into our organisation. There is a difficulty there because you have a lot of older people like me supervising a lot of younger people coming in who have very different needs.

We've gone down a disruptive learning route as well as our traditional management programmes, teaching them finances and strategy stuff and then sending them out to charities for a week so they can, for example, spend a night with homeless people. They then come back and innovate in a very different way because we force them to engage with very different people.

By doing that, we are trying to create the right kind of environment and the right management and leadership and culture to be able to bring people in who have very different values. If you want to innovate, if you want to co-create, we as organisations have to be much more flexible in the way we try to engage with people.

Consistency of application

In an age where generation Y and indeed a much broader spectrum of employees are becoming cynical about being "sold to" (see Chapter 4), the values espoused by companies that adopt a culture-led approach to talent management must be applied consistently.

Google has learned this lesson the hard way. From its inception, the company was the foremost champion of values-based engagement. Liane Hornsey, vice-president of people operations, argues that the company has turned its back on systems-led HR processes and planning in favour of the benefits gained from making the organisation both exciting and ethical. As she explains:

> Over I don't know how many years, I have learned one thing. And that one thing is that if you don't have a fertile soil in which you plant seeds, it doesn't matter how intellectually robust and how brilliant your processes and your programmes are, they will fail. But if you have a robust soil and a brilliant culture, the processes and the programmes can be pretty weak but they will work – because having the right culture is absolutely the bedrock to making sure you develop talent.

Google bases its culture on values and tenets summarised in Table 5.1. Hornsey stresses:

> We have 30,000 Googlers in more than 70 offices in over 40 countries. We operate in 112 languages and we have 157 international domains. In other words, we are big, we are global, we are everywhere. Every country knows Google exists. But if you walk into any one of those 70 Google offices, you know you are in Google. Every office might have its local flavour but they feel the same. And that is not by coincidence. We work it and we work it relentlessly and we work it really hard. We want to have one corporate culture. And that corporate culture is an environment in which we believe people thrive and people can develop.

Google has run into trouble on a number of occasions with regard to living up to its ten tenets. Examples have included its assault on copyright, privacy issues involving its street photography, the collection of private data, its cave-in to the authorities in China on censorship and, along with many other firms, the amount of tax it pays.

In the UK, the search engine has tumbled in the rankings of

TABLE 5.1 **Google values and tenets**
10 things we have found to be true

1	Focus on the user and all else will follow
2	It's best to do one thing really, really well
3	Fast is better than slow
4	Democracy on the web works
5	You don't need to be at your desk to need an answer
6	You can make money without doing evil
7	There is always more information out there
8	The need for information crosses all borders
9	You can be serious without a suit
10	Great just isn't good enough

brands compiled from a survey of 12,000 consumers by Clear, a brand research and strategy consultancy owned by M&C Saatchi, an international advertising agency. Google was named the fifth most desirable brand by Britons in the same survey in 2012, but new figures published in July 2013 reveal that it has fallen out of the top 20. Furthermore, the Wikipedia entry "Criticisms of Google" now stretches to 25 pages.

It is too early to assess how much, if at all, this will affect Google's ability to attract and retain talented staff – but it will certainly put some people off the idea of working for the company.

The need for transparency

The most important prerequisite for culture-led approaches is that the organisation should be entirely transparent about its talent management processes. Difficult decisions must always be made about who is designated as talent, and it is better for people to understand why they have been left out rather than suspecting it is because of nepotism or behind-the-scenes politicking, which would undermine any claims by the company to value talent.

How transparent organisations should be about who they mark out as talented is hotly debated. Most companies do not tell prospective candidates that they are in the talent management system and are viewed as talent. Some are opaque, indicating that an individual is viewed as talented but not saying much about how their career will be managed as a consequence.

Research by the Chartered Institute of Personnel and Development in 2010 suggests that organisations with a "hidden" system are often worried that:

- their method of selecting talented people and progressing their careers is not robust enough, and thus could be subject to challenge;
- being open about their opinion of an individual's potential will encourage unrealistic expectations about salary and promotion, and even encourage the individual to recognise their talent and start looking for jobs in competing organisations;
- being open about who is regarded as talented would have a demotivating impact on those not identified.

Ashridge explored the issue of transparency in a 2007 online survey of 1,500 UK-based managers. Although the results indicated that only 7% of managers believed being identified as talented resulted in resentment among peers, the report posed the same question as the CIPD research:

> Do you tell people they are considered talented in order to be honest, boost their confidence, focus their career and increase their engagement but risk that they become arrogant, feel overpressured and have an inflated sense of self-worth; or do you not tell people they are considered talented, leaving them to guess what the organisation thinks of them and losing the benefits that can be gained from their knowing?

One solution, suggested the report, is to have a talent management system where there is a constant movement of talent in and out of the talent pool, so that the title of talented is not a permanent label. Organisations would design their system so that people move in and out of the talent pool at different career stages, re-entering it when they are ready for the next stage, major job move or promotion.

This can help reduce the distinction of talent and non-talent (it is just where you are in your career stage) and take the pressure off someone who is not in a position to benefit from the opportunities of being in the pool (for example, because of family or personal responsibilities). It also makes it easier to deal with those whose "talent" turns into arrogance or fails to live up to expectations. And late or slow developers are more likely to eventually find their place in the pool.

The view of Marielle de Macker, HR managing director at Randstad, is fairly typical of the managers interviewed for this book. Randstad has a talent pool for the top 1,000 positions in the global company and attempts to identify the top 200 in the pool and actively develop them. De Macker comments:

> We have a structured mechanism in place to calibrate our talent continuously against each other, and have an up to date view on their drive, judgment and influencing skills, which for us are good indicators of their future potential.

Asked whether the company tells people whether they are in the pool, she replies:

> Not always, but I think we should. In today's world of openness and transparency people are entitled to know where they are and how they are being viewed and they should be invited to think about any improvement or development actions if needed.

It is difficult to see how a culture based on openness and transparency can be sustained if an organisation's opinion of its workers is hidden or at best opaque. Even if companies decide to tell individuals that they are rated highly, it is still likely that their colleagues will notice that they are receiving special attention from senior managers as well as extra development opportunities and work experiences.

A personal or tailored approach to promotion and career management of the kind described in Chapter 4 would be impossible to sustain. Furthermore, the lack of a frank exchange about an individual's prospects in the organisation would fail to alert senior managers to those who do not want to be in "the system", may not aspire to top jobs or whose personal circumstances may make it impossible for them to be (either temporarily or permanently) internationally or regionally mobile.

Ross Hall, who has been a member of the talent pool at both GlaxoSmithKline, a multinational pharmaceuticals company, and Pearson, a multinational publishing and education company, supports this view. He has some searching questions about whether talent pools can really provide the more personal approach that people like him increasingly want:

I wonder if the concept of talent pools is redundant and ineffective. What I am not sure of is whether it is the management of talent pools that is at fault or whether it is the concept itself. It would be interesting to know what the typical size of a talent pool is because the reality is that you are restricted in the number of people you can really give opportunity to. What does opportunity look like? Is it what we as a company want or is it what the individual wants?

The idea that we are trying to find something that suits an individual's purpose and the organisation's purpose immediately suggests that it has to be something personal. Otherwise what we want to do with talented people generically is by definition not personal and not what the individual wants to get out of it themselves.

By definition it must be personal and we are therefore very restricted from a resource perspective in terms of the number of people we can manage in this way. Then you have a real problem because you have to say how many people can be managed and if it is one person that doesn't constitute a pool. If you have a pool of 100 people but you can only manage two or three people at the end of it, what you need is a very rigorous but very transparent filtering process.

This is the whole argument for the need for talent management to be personal because those of us running a business have particular things we want to achieve. We have corporate objectives that we want to achieve through the nurturing of talent. What is very, very rarely done in my experience is any substantial conversation with the individual to say what do you want to achieve?

What I don't like about it is that I am named as part of a talent pool and that leads to strained relationships with people who aren't in the talent pool. There is also this idea that if you are in the talent pool, you get to network with other talented people – but who is defining talent? Are you saying that anybody who is left out of the talent pool has no talent?

It raises a lot of questions, not least of which is shouldn't companies make a talent pool voluntary and let people put themselves forward for promotion?

Conclusion

If companies want to recruit and retain the best-performing employees, they need to espouse cultural values and goals which go beyond merely appealing to these individuals. There needs to be a more fundamental emotional connection where gifted individuals personally identify with the organisation and believe they can make a difference by working there. Senior managers play a vital role in "bonding" talent to the organisation by making time to get to know such individuals and showing how much the company values their contribution. This culturally based engagement can help a company through good and bad times. It can be the key to retaining crucial staff during periods of slow growth, with all the bottlenecks in promotion and unrealisable expectations that occur in such circumstances.

Failure to live up to the high standards of probity and integrity that an organisation has set itself, and that form the most important contribution to its "employer brand", can also have a detrimental effect on its talent management strategy.

A culture-led approach has some dangers, however. Companies can become so obsessed by the idea of achieving a tight cultural "fit" between the organisation and the individual that they become risk adverse in their recruitment and selection decisions. The organisation misses out on individuals who are motivated differently, but who nonetheless have valuable skills to offer, such as highly creative people or entrepreneurs. The next chapter looks at how firms can capitalise on individuals who have opted out of a traditional career or who have been ignored because they worked at the periphery of the organisation in part-time, contract or associate roles.

6   Creating a talent ecosystem

If you join McKinsey, you join for life even though you are not
necessarily still employed here.
>   Emily Lawson, head of global human capital practice,
>   McKinsey & Company

As this book has already touched upon in Chapters 1 and 4,
companies rarely have a clear strategy on how to make the most of:

- creative and innovative mavericks and outsiders;
- those who are entrepreneurially minded and usually leave
  because they are frustrated by the lack of opportunity to engage in
  start-up activities. There are also those who (more cynically) use a
  corporate career as a stepping stone to launch their own enterprise;
- late starters or those people recruited later in their careers who
  might be considered gap fillers rather than potential high-flyers;
- those who would like to make and would respond well to a
  sideways move, or those who want to make sideways moves for
  personal reasons or because they prefer the line of work;
- those who are deterred by the price that has to be paid to climb
  the corporate ladder.

This is costing organisations dear because a growing proportion of
the flexible, agile and creative people they require to anticipate and
respond effectively to change fall into one or more of these categories.

The cause of this failure lies in an outdated model of strategic
workforce planning that emerged in the 1980s. This divides the
organisation into a "core" of "firm-specific" workers and managers

who are the focus for promotion and development. At the growing "periphery" of the organisation are part-time, contract and associate staff who are recruited because they are cheaper to employ and whose careers and aspirations are largely ignored.

The second orthodoxy is a concept of retention that equates with continued permanent employment inside the organisation, at a time when the idea of committing themselves to a lifetime career in a single organisation is neither realistic nor desirable to talented people.

This chapter argues that companies have the option to broaden access to their talent by being less rigid in their thinking and freer, more imaginative and less possessive in their approach to talent people.

Career planning and intrapreneurs

In the mid-1980s, Marsha Sinetar, a researcher at the Massachusetts Institute of Technology, undertook a survey of intrapreneurs – people with entrepreneurial spirit and aspirations who choose to work inside large corporations. Her study of hundreds of managers with a track record of successful entrepreneurial thinking and activity revealed that they had the following things in common:

- They are easily bored, and would rather move into untried areas.
- They are comfortable with ambiguous situations.
- They are happy to take risks – and indeed enjoy doing so.
- They are intellectually curious, needing to use their minds to solve difficult, personally fulfilling problems.
- They often see their work as a calling or vocation.

Intrapreneurs, Sinetar argued, possess personalities that thrive on freedom in three important areas: freedom in the general area of their work and the way in which work gets done; freedom to come up with novel or disturbing questions; and freedom to come up with unusual solutions to the things they are currently thinking about, sometimes in the form of what seem, to others, to be impractical ideas. At the same time, she found that this singular thinking often undermined their ability to work in teams, supervise other staff or lead the organisation.

This creates a dilemma for the conventional career planning that is often a feature of talent management strategies. Unless organisations can meet the need presented by these freedoms, they are liable to lose the individual to ones that can.

The warning is amplified by Tim Levine, who gave up a traditional corporate career to pursue a life as an entrepreneur in his 20s and is now a managing partner and founder of a venture capital firm, Augmentum Capital. As he explains:

> If a company's entrepreneurial talent is not being challenged, they are going to get frustrated and bored and look elsewhere. This has always been the case, but the options for corporations are more limited in the current climate of expectation and aspirations than they were.
>
> Some of these options might involve moving these talented people across the organisation or giving them new roles and opportunities that make them feel they are growing.
>
> A company might well have subsidiaries in other companies where they can put their talent into senior positions, which gives them that learning opportunity and the opportunity to act independently.
>
> On the other hand, you could do something drastic, which some corporations are doing, which is to create spin-off enterprises which offer more entrepreneurial people the chance to play with a fully capitalised new business.
>
> For me, the time when I am learning is when I am enjoying the greatest levels of satisfaction. This might involve making mistakes or learning from people more experienced than myself.
>
> You might argue today that in the economic environment people are going to be hard pressed to find good jobs elsewhere – but the crème will always find the best jobs. Many will take the risk of leaving their employer if they have a strong belief in themselves. So you cannot be complacent.

Stephen Dury, managing director of strategy and market development at Santander UK, is a good example of what Levine is talking about. He moved on from a career at Royal Bank of Scotland to join Santander. He was attracted to the Spanish bank because he believed it had an entrepreneurial culture and was willing to be innovative, targeting in particular small and medium-sized enterprise (SME) and start-up customers.

> I am a marketer by background and education. I have a keen interest and passion for new market development, innovation, disruptive technology and learning from the way SMEs and entrepreneurs behave. Lots of innovation comes from SMEs.
>
> I knew of Santander because I knew some of the people that had moved there – very good people – and you would hear that people were creating great opportunities in a creative, structured and entrepreneurial environment. Going into a business where there are very clear lines of accountability, space for innovation and sponsorship from the senior executive team makes any business more attractive – this is a culture that fosters creativity and delivery in equal measure.

The work Dury undertakes at Santander – including developing new ideas and services for start-ups and SMEs – puts him into contact with a wide variety of entrepreneurs, something that provides him with significant job satisfaction.

> I love working with entrepreneurs. I'm fortunate to work on and be responsible for a lot of entrepreneurial projects. I've thought a lot about the way I try to approach challenges and it is similar to the way some entrepreneurs approach running their own businesses. I try to think of them as role models in the way in which they make decisions – their creative thinking, passion and dedication is inspiring.
>
> Entrepreneurs think they are part of the solution and no matter what gets thrown at them they find a way of doing things differently or overcoming the challenge they face. They are confident and unwavering in their focus to make things happen and it's this drive that makes them successful. This entrepreneurial spirit and tenacity is not something I believe everybody has.

Business incubation

Some intrapreneurs will never be happy with the opportunities offered by a traditional corporate career.

Ross Hall is a good example. He was headhunted by Pearson, a multinational publishing and education company with headquarters in London, on the basis of his background in setting up new businesses. He says:

> They particularly wanted someone who could come in and take a fresh perspective on this particular business unit and to see if it could be turned around.

However, his restless mind and social conscience led him to explore other avenues for his talent. With Pearson, a company that has a strong commitment and business in developing new education materials, he looked at developing a new form of schooling in rural Zimbabwe and Tanzania. This involved extending the traditional curriculum beyond normal subjects to develop qualities of mind that are most influential in creating and maintaining quality of life, with topics such as empathy, assertiveness and self-esteem.

Hall realised that this was a step too far for Pearson and that his senior management colleagues did not have the appetite for the project, which led him to consider pursuing the idea on his own. He was appreciative of Pearson allowing him to explore the idea using its resources, but the impasse caused him to consider a deeper philosophical question about intrapreneurialism:

> I have a very live question, which is: "Do companies really want people like me?" I think there is a lot of recognition that companies could benefit from having people like me. But the reality is that entrepreneurial people are difficult to manage and the value that they bring is not always immediate – these things take a long time to develop. They can also cause friction with the main business when they try to do things differently. Does the company really have the appetite and ability to execute their new ideas?

Hall is not the only person asking this question. At a talent summit in 2012, Khurshed Dehnugara, author of *The Challenger Spirit:*

Organisations that Disturb the Status Quo, pointed out the contradiction between what organisations say and do when attempting to meet the aspirations of intrapreneurs.

He argues that that companies send out messages that encourage staff to be creative, disruptive and risk-taking while at the same time punishing people who "mess up and fail to keep everything nice and stable". As he concludes:

> *Faced with this contradiction, people take up the default position of staying safe so that nothing can go wrong. My concern is that future talent is desperate for something more groundbreaking.*

Some telecoms and digital companies have accommodated the entrepreneurial aspirations of their most talented intrapreneurs and those of people they would not normally attract by setting up business incubation schemes, offering start-up funding to help them create their own enterprises. This offer of help is in return for a stake in the business or access to the new technology or thinking of the start-up.

This is an effective way of extending the organisation's reach to young entrepreneurs who have opted out of corporate employment. As Tim Levine observes:

> *I started having a conventional corporate career – but it all felt very bureaucratic and restrictive.*
>
> *What I started to see were new technologies coming on board and what I hoped would happen was that the next generation of entrepreneurs would be empowered by new platforms such as the internet, which it certainly has been. That has changed the whole dynamic of young graduates with aspirations to be an entrepreneur. It is a hell of a lot easier now than 10–15 years ago. You are empowered.*
>
> *In the 1980s if you were talented and entrepreneurial, you needed capital and you needed large office space. Today you can create a website if you have a good idea and your requirement of capital is minimal. There has been a huge shift of ambition among young people of school leaving age. If I told my father when I left university that I was not going into conventional business but I was*

*going to be an entrepreneur, he would have thought I was going to
be unemployed for the next three or four years.*

*It is now a much more acceptable path for people leaving
university or even school to have this ambition. They are no longer
regarded as mavericks. There are probably lots of people in their
early 20s building really successful businesses. The barriers to entry
are nowhere near as considerable as they were. I think that is a real
challenge for corporations. The ambition is there and these people
do not want to be pigeon-holed.*

*There is a greater level of impatience among talented young
people and if they are not getting what they want, they are going to
leave. It doesn't mean that they will be successful and won't come
back, but the question for corporations is what they do with these
ambitious young people. Do you encourage them? Do you try to
incubate them? There are a lot of options.*

The most well-developed incubation initiative is the Wayra
Academy, the brainchild of José María Alvarez-Pallete, chairman and
chief executive of Telefónica Europe. This provides start-ups with
€50,000 in funding in return for a 10% stake, and Telefónica gets the
right of first refusal on buying the company.

It was originally launched in Latin America and Spain, where
there are nine business incubation schemes, and has been more
widely extended in Europe. At its London offices, for example, Wayra
accommodates about 20 start-ups for six months, after which it will
help them pitch for follow-on funding from other sources of venture
capital. If a start-up does not find other sources of funding in six
months, it may be granted another six months. If after that things are
still not working out, Wayra will sell its stake for €1.

Simon Devonshire, manager of Wayra's London offices, took the
unusual step of selling the idea in bars, clubs and coffee houses. As
he explains:

*Entrepreneurs are quite a difficult bunch to identify. I can't think of
a conventional advertising medium you could use. I have always
been passionately obsessed about networking and informal means
of connectivity. If you send the right message out and you have the*

*right touch points, the first respondents become ambassadors for the
project.*

*The first night we tried it, our people at Telefónica went nuts,
saying we would only get 12 people. It netted us 30 people. The next
time we got 50 people. By the fourth time out we had 300 people.
The word soon spread and the numbers grew in leaps and bounds.
The bars were really an instrument of that strategy rather than being
the strategy itself.*

Telefónica Europe plans to open other Wayra Academies in Berlin,
Dublin and Prague. Ultimately it plans to fund around 350 start-ups. As
Devonshire argues, Wayra is as much a part of its talent management
strategy as its high-potential schemes for senior managers, extending
its reach far further than most of its competitors:

*It is not just about the ideas. It is about attracting talented people. We
are using Wayra as a way of acquiring great talent for the benefit
of Telefónica. And like many talent management schemes, we bring
mentors into the academy to help and support and realise their best
potential.*

Linked-in internships

Both Santander UK and Telefónica recruit interns for their start-up
schemes from Enternships, an online company that finds places in
SMEs for university graduates with entrepreneurial ambitions. For
example, Enternships has a partnership with Santander to supply
interns for the bank's SME customers, linked to the Santander
Universities Programme, which embraces 60 universities and funds
500 internships.

As Rajeeb Dey, the founder and CEO of Enternships, explains,
the enterprise enables companies to contact and build relationships
with young talent who would otherwise not think of working in a
conventional employee relationship:

*Companies, big and small, need people who are entrepreneurial or
think like an entrepreneur – that is the ability to spot opportunities,
to take risks and to hit the ground running.*

The world is moving fast, and companies need people who are able to adapt quickly, who are agile and can operate in a time of flux and help the business grow. In a start-up, these qualities are obvious because you are part of a small team, everybody needs to pull their weight and there is no space for dead wood.

You will be spotted quickly if you are not adding value. At the same time, large corporations are spotting that they need entrepreneurial talent within their organisation. But the challenge is that corporate structures may not be right to enable the talent to flourish because in order to have truly entrepreneurial talent, you need to enable risk-taking and give a level of autonomy and freedom. Because of the way many reporting systems and appraisals work, a large company is not conducive to a truly entrepreneurial and maverick individual.

Having said that, the spectrum of entrepreneurial skill is broad. There is the through-and-through entrepreneur who you would struggle to get into a corporate environment (like myself). Then you have people who have entrepreneurial aspirations or tendencies yet crave the comfort of security and structure around them – and therefore would be more of an intrapreneur.

Companies, big and small, need to identify the individuals who will keep the business one step ahead, spawn new opportunities and help the company to grow.

Schemes like Enternships are important because the proportion of young people with entrepreneurial ambitions is increasing.

In the United States, a nationwide cell-phone and landline survey, conducted by the Young Invincibles in 2011 in conjunction with Lake Research Partners and Bellwether Research and funded by the Ewing Marion Kauffman Foundation, polled 872 "millennials" (young people aged between 18 and 25) on their thoughts about the economy and entrepreneurship.

Carl Schramm, president and chief executive of the Kauffman Foundation, says:

This poll reveals a generation that is enthusiastic about entrepreneurship, and that is good news for the US; 54% of the nation's millennials either want to start a business or already have started one. They recognise that entrepreneurship is the key to reviving the economy.

An even higher percentage of young people from ethnic minorities – 64% of Latinos and 63% of African-Americans – expressed a desire to start their own companies.

However, despite young people's strong entrepreneurial drive, just 8% of the people polled owned businesses at the time of the survey, and only 11% intended to start businesses within the next year; 38% of the potential young entrepreneurs said they had delayed starting a business because of the economy.

Aaron Smith, co-founder and executive director of Young Invincibles, says:

An astounding number of young people want to start a business one day. And they overwhelmingly support action on the part of their leaders to remove barriers to these dreams.

The poll highlights specific barriers to entrepreneurship, including the inability to access the capital needed to get a business going, a lack of knowledge needed to run a small business, concerns with overcoming current debt burdens and a lack of mentors from whom young people can learn.

Some 65% of the people polled think that making it easier to start a business should be a priority for Congress, with 41% saying it should be a top priority; 83% believe that Congress should, at a minimum, increase the availability of start-up loans. Even more respondents – 92% – support increased access to the education and training needed to run a small business as a way to encourage people to become entrepreneurs, and 81% support student loan relief for young people who start companies.

Alumni and associates

Organisations should be seeking to create an "ecosystem" that enables them to have access to the skills of young entrepreneurs who do not want to follow a conventional corporate career. Retaining relationships with talented people who leave organisations in mid-career and do not aspire to corporate leadership roles is also crucial.

Large management consultancies such as Accenture, McKinsey and the Boston Consulting Group are champions of the idea that former employees should be seen as and encouraged to see themselves as "alumni" of the organisation. They take the pragmatic and realistic view that at least 50% of the consultants they recruit will leave the organisation within their first decade of employment, either to pursue a corporate career or to set up their own enterprise.

Far from attempting to handcuff their staff, many consultancies actively encourage their corporate or entrepreneurial ambitions on the grounds that they will wind up being future clients or collaborators, bringing in new business to their former "alma mater".

As Emily Lawson of McKinsey explains:

> We constantly challenge and review our processes to try to ensure that we are bringing in the best, managing them well and offering them fantastic opportunities and ensuring that they feel good about the firm, whether or not they decide to stay or go. We manage our alumni network very actively.
>
> So if you join McKinsey, you join for life even though you are not necessarily still employed here. We manage much less through systems and much more through values. Our risk management systems are about embedding a common set of values and holding that very visibly. There is a set of norms about how you behave that are well understood and are inculcated early on within your first year.

Tim Levine found this was also true of Bain & Company, a global management consulting firm, for which he worked before pursuing an entrepreneurial career. As he explains:

> They certainly don't hold you back. They take the attitude that if you are going to leave, you are going to leave. They take pride in the success of their alumni and in my case, they allowed me to continue to work in the office and use it as a resource centre – and keep my desk for a period of six months. This was critical for me when I was setting something up and short of capital.
>
> It is also hard to work on your own and you have plenty of smart people around you. It really helps the transition. And they

were keen for me to know that if the enterprise didn't work out, my old job with them was still there. They stated frequently that they would love to have me back but at the same time they wished me every success in my endeavours to be an entrepreneur. That is a very nice position to be in.

More generally, there has been an increase in former employees working in associate and consultancy positions for their one-time employers. A new breed of well-qualified and highly motivated freelancers called independent professionals or IPros are choosing self-employment for its own merits rather than seeing it as second-best option because full-time work is not available.

As the foremost researcher on IPros, Patricia Leighton, emeritus professor of employment at the University of Glamorgan, explains:

If we define IPros in terms of high skill and generally a high level of educational attainment and then disaggregate them from the general statistics on self-employment, they are a dramatically increasing element of both the UK and EU labour market. It has been recently reported that between 2008 and 2011, their numbers increased by 12.5%. In some EU states the growth has been well in excess of that. For the UK, the figure is 24%, accounting for over 1.6m people in 2011.

Moreover, there is no research evidence that supports the idea that these people are forced into IPro work due to lack of permanent employment. Generally, they have freely chosen to work this way and equally importantly, regularly conducted surveys from the UK, Netherlands and Australia tell the same story, that many have rejected standard employment.

They tend to dislike working in bureaucratic, hierarchical organisations and especially "office gossip and backstabbing". They seek autonomy. Their commitment is to their skill or occupation and not to an individual employer.

Leighton stresses that reports on IPros suggest that they have high levels of job satisfaction and self-respect and that they feel valued by clients and collaborators. "They look forward to Monday mornings," she comments.

Moreover, although IPros were traditionally male and moved into self-employment after a career as an ordinary employee, the latest EU research from the Nordic states, Germany and the Netherlands demonstrates that a growing number go straight into self-employment after studying for graduate and postgraduate qualifications – and that women make up a growing proportion of this group. As Leighton comments:

> This is interesting because this is probably before they have got children or have other caring responsibilities. In other words, there is a growing number who are saying "actually, this is the way I do want to work. I don't want to work in a large organisation". This is a significant development. The average age of IPros is going down. Most of them will not say that they will never work as an employee. They are saying this is their preferred choice.

Conclusion

Every organisation should consider how it can widen its access to talent. The proportion of employees who will do what it currently takes to climb the corporate ladder is shrinking and what used to be termed "the periphery" is growing. People at the periphery consist of those who have opted for part-time, self-employed or contract work from choice and not necessity and who possess skills that previously would have been confined to the core.

There are also growing numbers of young people who are opting out of corporate employment and whose skills and entrepreneurial flair are needed by the companies they are forsaking.

Within large corporations, there are mavericks, intrapreneurs and specialists who are not catered for by traditional talent management programmes but who, again, have skills that are increasingly relevant to an uncertain commercial environment.

The use of business incubation schemes and linked-in internships, career planning specifically targeted at intrapreneurs, and relationships with former employees based on the concept of alumni and associate status enables organisations to widen their access to talent.

This all requires fresh thinking and a new, more flexible approach. Caroline Curtis, head of talent, succession and leadership development at Santander UK, observes that this means opening up the talent management programme and focusing more on enabling the business units to assess and evaluate their own talented individuals in terms of their strengths, aspirations and future potential.

Stephen Dury of Santander UK concludes:

> When I am given an innovative, challenging project, which is about developing a new proposition, changing the business or shaping the organisation, often what I am looking for within the business are intrapreneurs and talented people from all backgrounds that feel an individual responsibility for doing things better and want to help make a difference.
>
> The challenge is identifying those people who might not appear on our talent map but you know from working with them that they fit the talent profile that is needed within Santander. It is also about finding the talent that might not be available to you in your own organisation – and finding it at the right time and collaborating effectively for the benefit of everyone concerned. That can catapult talented people into a place where they want to stay.

Playing the talent game

*I think the issue of confidence does affect a lot of people and
for me this is about not being afraid to take risks. You need the
confidence to say I'm going to try this and not be afraid to fail.*
Rain Newton-Smith, head of emerging markets,
Oxford Economics

Shalini Joseph, who is in her 30s, has moved around a lot since she
graduated from the National Law School of India University in 2006.
She was recruited as a management trainee by a multinational fast-
moving consumer goods (FMGC) company, where she negotiated
and drafted contracts relating to the business and advised the
marketing and sales department about legal issues. A year later
she took up a short-term research internship at the Competition
Commission of India, a national antitrust regulatory body, where
she stayed for ten months. She then joined a leading Indian law
firm. Joseph says:

> *I was trying out things to find out what I really liked. I guess that
> was where there was a bit of a discrepancy between what I expected
> and what I finally got. That's where the movement happened.*

Meeting her career expectations was tough going for the companies
that employed her. As she explains:

> *When the FMCG company presented on campus, it sounded really
> exciting. The people who came were not so much from the legal
> department. They were from HR and marketing – and it sounded
> really good.*

Once I started working for the company in its law department, I realised that it wasn't fulfilling my aspirations because it was just a support function and that moving into core management in the firm wasn't possible. At that stage, I also felt I should be learning more. If you are not learning, and all your college peers are charging ahead and doing high-level deals, you feel the need to move.

The initial training programme gave me a holistic view of the business, but after that my work was nothing like it. Fresh out of school, it wasn't a challenge for me and challenge is important at that stage of your career. You need a stronger prospect of where the job is going to lead. It made me feel it's going to take forever to get anywhere. My feeling was that in some law firms, if you can prove yourself, you can move up really fast. That is a huge motivation factor.

Joseph worked for almost three years at Trilegal, a law firm in Mumbai. Then an old dream of doing an MBA came back and she decided to apply. She was offered a place at INSEAD in November 2010 and immediately quit Trilegal. This turned out to be a mistake, as personal and financial circumstances forced her to turn down the offer and defer her MBA by almost a year.

During that year she travelled and also worked for a non-governmental organisation, where she got her first taste of entrepreneurship and business management. That experience is what really cemented her decision to pursue a career in management. As she explains:

I originally had an interest in marketing which I put on hold. I found in law that it was executing the business end of transactions that I was missing out on. So I figured let's take this one step further. There are so many things in business I could do but I didn't need to decide what I would end up in. An MBA makes perfect sense to help me decide that. It could be marketing, it could be consulting, it could be private equity. One year doing an MBA studying these subjects would help me figure that out.

The thought, research and analysis Joseph put into her career is not unusual. Playing the talent game requires risk-taking, opportunism and bags of self-confidence. It also requires people to make the grade in the organisations they work for and negotiate their way through career paths that, as Chapter 4 outlined, look more like trellises or even labyrinths than old-fashioned ladders.

Making the company grade

The first challenge is to meet the targets that an organisation sets. As indicated in Chapter 1, most businesses measure high potential in terms of each individual meeting two interlocking criteria:

- the ability to hit performance targets;
- the ability to demonstrate senior management potential.

Delivering against performance targets is easy to quantify. Most organisations operate some form of performance management process that assesses on a regular basis each person's (or team's) ability to meet set targets. Targets are usually set in advance and subject to quarterly or annual appraisals so, provided the targets are sufficiently defined, it is not difficult to assess whether someone is at the grade or not.

Demonstrating potential is more problematic. First, the criteria used to assess leadership potential vary and will be shaped by an organisation's remit, culture and strategy. Second, organisations are often far less transparent about what they mean by "potential" than what they mean by performance. Individuals may have to deploy some educated guesswork or detective work to assess where they are in the pecking order.

Google's means of assessing potential provides some clues. Unlike many organisations, it is fairly transparent about the criteria it uses. These were outlined at a talent summit in 2012 by Liane Hornsey, vice-president of people operations:

> We measure leadership against five criteria. Being Google, we didn't take those five criteria off the shelf. No. We took all the data from our attitude surveys in the last five years, all the data from our upward feedback surveys since they began and all our performance data – and we looked for trends about what makes a great leader. We also did a great many in-depth interviews with those leaders

that we deemed to be great on paper and those leaders that we deemed to be pretty damn awful on paper – and we interviewed a lot of their direct reports too.

In that way, looking at qualitative and quantitative Google-based data, we came up with five capabilities for senior leaders. They are simple and some of them you would easily recognise but they are important.

The first one obviously – it sounds like a "motherhood and apple pie" statement but it is so important – is to be able to lead people with vision. This is about alignment and engagement. No question in Google. If you haven't got the heart, forget the mind.

The second thing is we measure our leaders on their ability to collaborate across functions. We believe in teams, and we believe in teams within teams within teams. We don't like politicking. So I could be a phenomenal leader within my own team, score brilliantly according to my upward feedback surveys, but if my 360-degree feedback says that somebody over here thinks I am a jerk, I'm not doing very well when it comes to my performance. So we look for people who can really collaborate in a genuine way.

Third, we look for people who can make timely decisions through periods of ambiguity. This is important to us because we have a lot of engineers who always want the data. We have to balance emotional intelligence and IQ when it comes to decision-making. So we do a lot of work to try to make sure that people can use their gut instincts as well as their head. The head always leads in Google but the guts are important too. When we look at achieving whole person development, that is what we focus on.

The fourth capability is the ability to develop teams to succeed. So if your upward feedback is rubbish, you are not going to do well in your performance management. If your teams are not singing because you are the leader, you are not going to do well.

Finally, we measure people on their ability to deliver results in times of change.

Google's way of assessing these leadership traits is also revealing. As Hornsey explains:

Google is an analytical company. We measure everything. And the People Operations Function is no different. This is the most analytical function I have ever worked in. We do nothing without an algorithm. So, how do we determine whether our people are very good? We absolutely measure our leadership capability.

Twice a year every single manager or leader throughout the organisation has upward feedback. It is quite an onerous process. Every single person in the organisation is asked to comment on their manager.

On top of that, we have an attitude survey once a year. So, again, we ask our people to comment on their managers. And then we stack-rank all our managers and leaders and instead of chastising the bottom 20%, we sit them down – we try not to make it clear that they are in the bottom 20% – but the bottom 20% will be coached by the HR business partners.

Every single person in the bottom 20% will see the HR business partner naturally in the course of events. They'll talk through their survey, they'll talk through their strengths, they'll talk through their weaknesses and they'll be coached and supported.

And then, by the way, because we value behaviours and we value the way people act, we link improvement to objectives – and we link objectives to pay. So we put our money where our mouth is. You get better as a leader, you get more pay.

Being opportunistic

The last thing worth noting about Google's way of assessing senior management potential is that it places a premium on people who take risks. As Hornsey concludes:

One of the things we ask our people to do is think big, be innovative and have ideas – and not just having ideas but bringing teams and people together and implementing your idea. What does this do to the talent development agenda? Of course, it identifies your stars without you having to do a thing and without you having to hunt for them. All you have to do is to provide an environment where people are willing to take risks. Of course, as in all walks of life, the cream rises to the top.

This is a fundamental rule of thumb for aspiring senior managers even when it is not appreciated by the organisation. The one thing that marked out the managers interviewed for this book with a successful track record of career success was their willingness to be opportunistic and take risks.

Rain Newton-Smith, head of emerging markets at Oxford Economics and in 2012 named as one of the World Economic Forum's "Young Global Leaders", took full advantage of the potentially risky opportunities she was presented with. First, she accepted a role as economic adviser to Sir Richard Lambert when he was one of the nine members of the Monetary Policy Committee of the Bank of England, which sets UK interest rates. Second, she accepted a secondment to the IMF because she wanted to focus her career on analysing emerging economies. In both cases, the decisions brought risks. As she explains:

> When I went to the job as adviser to Richard Lambert, that was seen as a risky move because I had the potential to follow the very traditional Bank of England route of taking internal jobs and working my way up the hierarchy. I chose instead a job where I wouldn't have the same support structure but had the potential for a hugely rewarding role.
>
> It did really pay off and then the opportunity for the secondment to the IMF came up when I had only been in the job as an adviser for a year. You are visible in those roles and setting up the roles of external advisers had created tensions between the internal and the external members of the Monetary Policy Committee.
>
> There was still a bit of a fall-out from that. But I went into it saying this is ridiculous, we were all working essentially towards the same goal and this is the way I am going to tackle this. I think that straightforward approach worked. Also it was a job I really enjoyed. Jobs you enjoy, you do well.

Newton-Smith's philosophy is that you should grab opportunities when they come your way:

> What people really value is individuals who have worked in different places. If you don't take these opportunities, you never

know what might happen to you further down the line. For me, the role of adviser was brilliant and I had a fantastic time. That role gave me a lot of confidence and gave me a very good skill set – and in terms of my Bank of England career, was very good. In terms of the secondment to the IMF, it might have been a bit of a trade-off in terms of if you stay at the Bank, you might get promoted internally a little bit quicker than if you go out.

In fact, many managers interviewed for this book stressed that people should not be constrained by over-rigid career plans, whether prescribed by the organisation they are working for or of their own making.

Ian Pearman, chief executive of Abbott Mead Vickers, observes:

I think it helps not having a long-term plan about your career. That kind of plan can create behaviours that are counter-productive, particularly for future managers and leaders. You end up trying to be pulled up rather than pushed up.

If you are focused on the next job, then by definition you have to focus on being the very best in your current job. That kind of relatively focused ambition probably leads to behaviours that will be more admired and respected in the long term.

I have seen people who, because they are so intent on getting up the ladder as soon as possible, have only looked upwards and have done anything possible to be pulled up. So they have been much more concerned about managing their boss than managing their peers or managing their subordinates.

This is a sustainable strategy up to a certain point but the point when you run out of road is the point where everybody you need hates you because they are below you and you have never looked after them. You need to understand that your success is completely conditional on the respect and the trust you develop in those that work for you and around you.

Developing a support network

Another characteristic that marks out successful managers is their ability to build and maintain a support network, both inside and outside their organisation. As Pearman observes:

I was very lucky to have some very good mentors – they were not imposed on me. They were people that I sought out on how to navigate the challenges – people who could "course-correct" me.

The biggest factor was "not knowing what you don't know". It's about the combination of knowing what is the right question that you should be asking and how you get over the inevitable hump of not knowing what you don't know. My mentors served that purpose of taking me from unknown unknowns to known unknowns.

I use that phrase all the time in creating change management analogies when we are going into new markets and new disciplines. Finding people who can accelerate our learning and therefore reduce the risk of heinous mistakes is critical.

Newton-Smith also found her own hand-picked mentors an important source of advice in making crucial career decisions:

An organisation like the Bank of England is very traditional and conservative. In these circumstances, having the chance to talk to someone who is more senior to you and who has had the chance to experience different things when they are not your line manager can be hugely beneficial. People who are successful do build up a network of people they can turn to and with whom they bounce off ideas.

One of the male colleagues I started working with in my first job at the Bank was someone who believed in me right from the start. He's someone I have gone to in order to discuss career moves. And he has talked to me about his career moves.

One of my female managers was brilliant and very supportive, not only in saying that I was great but also in saying where I needed to improve. She would say "look I think you are very good at presentations but I find in this situation, you are not as good as you could be – here is someone I know who can provide you with training on this".

When I was working with the UK Monetary Policy Committee, Diane Julius, the chief economist at British Airways before she came to the Bank of England, was also a great support. Diane was brilliant at trying to encourage young women and used to meet with female economists for lunchtime networking events.

Job rotation and mobility

As earlier chapters have said, the heart of any talent development strategy is making sure that potential high-flyers get experience of:

- different specialist functions – finance, strategy, operations, human resources, marketing, etc;
- leading projects and teams that cut across and encompass different functions and businesses;
- different businesses within the organisation's portfolio;
- different geographical locations – and thus different cultures – within the organisation's portfolio;
- general management tasks and posts.

Doug Baillie, chief human resources officer at Unilever, for example, describes his company's talent management strategy thus:

> Unilever is a company that encourages people to get both breadth and depth. Over 60% of the top 100 leaders have worked in at least two geographies. Breadth is important because if you think about the world today, which is really very volatile, complex and ambiguous, we really need agile leaders who have breadth and wisdom to handle the amount of change that is taking place.

The likelihood is that if an organisation is large and diverse and employees are seeking advancement and promotion, they should expect to be moved around on a regular basis. Baillie is a typical example. He describes his career at Unilever:

> Take my own career. I started in South Africa as a sales and marketing graduate. I worked there for about seven years, starting at the bottom carrying a briefcase and finding out what it was like working at the coalface. I went to Australia on a customs secondment, came back to South Africa working with a sales director, then I was sent to the central headquarters to learn how the organisation works. I was an internal marketing consultant going around the geography helping to instil new brands and innovation.

I ran operations and projects in Africa and the Middle East,
central and eastern Europe, Russia and Turkey. I then went back
and ran the South African business, ran Africa and the Middle
East and then I was sent to India – a radical change from working
in Africa. I wound up running the South Asian region, which
was a huge cultural challenge for me and tested whether I had
the breadth to run a much bigger region and cluster. From there I
ended up running Europe and then to my surprise I wound up in
HR.

Clearly, job rotation on this scale has big implications for a
person's family and personal life – particularly in terms of bringing
up children and the care of elderly relatives. In certain circumstances,
this can be overcome by traditional expatriate packages involving
spouses. But in an age in which each spouse is pursuing their own
career, the decision to change schools (particularly during secondary
education) can have a big impact on a child's progress; and if the care
of elderly relatives is involved, the traditional approach is often no
longer appropriate.

This may require transparent and frank negotiation with the
organisation about when employees are happy to be mobile and
when they need to stay put – with all the personal and professional
trade-offs this may involve.

Research for this book suggests the more valued an employee
is, the more accommodating the organisation may be. As Chapter
4 demonstrated, the best companies are adopting a more personal
approach to career planning. PepsiCo and Unilever, for example, are
attempting to plan the progression of their top people up to ten years
ahead, in line with their personal and family needs.

MBA considerations

People who are seriously considering a career in business management
sooner or later should decide whether to study for an MBA or a
related masters' qualification.

The craze for MBAs has lessened since it reached its peak in
the 1990s, but the degree still provides a good foundation for three
possible career avenues, not all mutually exclusive:

- a senior management career in a large corporation;
- a career as an associate and then possibly a partner in a management consultancy;
- founding, owning and running an enterprise.

A full-time MBA requires a considerable commitment of time and money. It can take up to two years to complete, at a time when students may have significant family responsibilities and promotion prospects at work, and the total tuition and accommodation costs, at current rates, are anything between $50,000 and $80,000.

Commitment to a part-time or modular MBA can, in some senses, be even greater, because studying will be combined with full-time work responsibilities and eat into family or leisure time in the evenings and at weekends.

Studying for an MBA should provide:

- an opportunity to take time out to reflect on career options and consider changes in direction;
- the chance to take elective courses and internships that will allow these career options to be explored;
- the provision of general management skills to supplement and build on specialist expertise;
- exposure to the latest research and thinking in business management;
- the opportunity to build a diverse and international network of business contacts with people from different countries and professional backgrounds;
- the chance to augment salary if students sign up to a top management consultancy or apply for a general management position, thereby providing them with a financial return for their personal investment of time and money.

The opportunity to take time out to consider career options is one of the most important by-products of studying for an MBA. As Sandra Schwarzer, director of careers services at INSEAD, comments:

If you have someone who is returning to a similar position or a similar industry, for them the MBA often doesn't accelerate their career. For career changers, it opens a whole new world.

What we try to tell people who opt to change careers is that you have to demonstrate the strength of your learning curve because you are starting at zero. We offer life-long career services to our alumni.

One of the things people often do is come back to us for coaching throughout their careers. Half of these people change their jobs within three to four years after graduating and move somewhere else.

What we try to do in the year that they are with us is to teach them how to manage their career effectively, how to be self-aware. The professors give them not only the hard skills but the communication skills (for example, when a union leader comes in and threatens a strike how do you respond to that?) and we make them aware of the fact that if you are in command of your career you need regular time to think about what is it that you want and how do you get it, how do you maintain your learning and how do you continue to develop yourself.

Internships, secondments and sabbaticals

As organisations have become flatter, there are more opportunities to make sideways moves to pursue specialist skills and knowledge or personal interests, or to explore new career options, either at the start of a career or in mid-life. Indeed, companies are increasingly offering such opportunities in an effort to attract and retain the most talented people (see Chapter 4).

Internships

Internships are a good way of exploring career options. An internship is a short-term placement within a company, designed to give the intern hands-on experience working within a particular industry. This can be used as a bridge between study and employment, to find out whether a particular industry or company is of interest, or to start a career move into a new area. Internships are offered mainly to undergraduates or MBA students as an integral part of their studies (and with the help of the university's careers service), but they can be useful to people in mid-career as well.

For example, CRCC Asia, a provider of internships in China, offers 1–3 month internships starting every month all year round, linked to Chinese language programmes, to allow students and young people wanting to pursue international careers to gain practical experience of working in China.

Tingwei Tan, a student from Singapore studying at Leicester University in the UK, describes her experience of a one-month CRCC legal internship in Beijing:

> I came across an e-mail circulating in my university offering a summer internship programme in China. As I was always curious about the Chinese work environment and culture, I sent in my résumé without much hesitation, hoping to gain some invaluable experiences.
>
> Arriving three days before my internship, I was given ample time to settle down. CRCC's staff settled me in by introducing me to the other interns and providing all of us with a welcome package, which included a detailed map of Beijing, a sim card with value, a Chinese translated pronunciation booklet, a detailed address of our service apartment and office, contacts for their staff and much more!
>
> On my first day of work, a CRCC staff member took me to my office and introduced me to my supervising solicitor and buddy. My buddy spent an hour of her precious time to share with me the firm's core values, needs and goals, after which she took me for a tour around the office and introduced me to the other lawyers.
>
> In no time, I felt like I was part of the firm and not merely just an intern. I was kept busy on most days; I assisted my buddy with research, translation and drafting. One of the main deals that I assisted in was a mining investment in Zimbabwe. As most of the new rules and regulations set out by the governmental bodies in Zimbabwe were in English, I realised that the translated information that was made available for the Chinese lawyers and investors was not as comprehensive as the original documents.

Secondments

Further along the career path, there are opportunities to experience similar benefits through secondments, as Rain Newton-Smith did with the IMF, which proved invaluable in pursuit of her wish to become a specialist in emerging markets.

Recognising that their best people value time out like this, a growing number of organisations are now building secondments into high-potential career plans. PepsiCo is one example, as Indra Nooyi, chairman and chief executive, explains:

> Offer them creative projects linked to the company's future. It's disruptive but try. Allow them to do non-traditional things. Young people like to get involved with projects that make a difference to the world. We formed PepsiCorps, where we send high-potential people off for a month.
>
> We are allowing them to interact with us in non-traditional ways. That is as important as the financial linkage and we want to take pride and emotion home and bring it back the next day.

PepsiCorps is a month-long "performance with purpose" leadership development programme. It aims to give employees on-the-ground insights into societal challenges and allows them to use their talents and business skills to make a positive impact. In 2012, for example, a team of eight employees went to the south-west United States, partnering with local communities and organisations to focus on health and nutrition and sustainable agriculture.

Another team spent four weeks working on improving access to clean water in India, building on the clean-water work done by a pilot team in Ghana the year before. The pilot team also worked with local water boards to improve community access to clean water, developed a strategy to boost eco-tourism and taught hygiene in schools.

Some larger organisations advertise secondment positions on internal notice boards or intranet systems. However, most secondments result from a direct approach from the seconding organisation to the host company or an individual.

Catherine Armstrong, senior lecturer in American History at Manchester Metropolitan University, has published guidelines on how to manage secondments. She comments:

You will probably meet up with members of both your old and new teams to agree on a timetable and the particulars of your new role. This should take place openly and with your full agreement, so if you feel as though you are being kept in the dark, let your current manager know. There may be practical problems such as space needed and ongoing workload to manage that affect your transfer into the new team, so be prepared to wait.

It may be that during your time away from your original job, you still keep in touch with your old colleagues, making sure you stay up to speed on their work to ensure that you are able to slip back smoothly into your old job at the end of the secondment period.

You will struggle in your new job if you do not have the skills to carry it off, so make sure you plan your move carefully. Keep yourself fully informed of what will be expected of you by your new colleagues, otherwise you could have a miserable time and wish you had never bothered moving.

Equally, do not use secondment as a way to avoid a job you dislike. Even though secondment could open up new opportunities for you, for some period of time you will probably have to move back to your old team and this could be awkward if you are not comfortable returning to them.

Sabbaticals

Sabbaticals allow people to take time out to pursue personal interests and are not usually linked to an internal career-development programme.

Essentially a sabbatical is a system whereby companies allow their employees to take an extended period of leave above their usual holiday allowance, with the guarantee that their job will be held open for them when they return. A sabbatical might be for a year but could equally be for, say, three or six months.

To qualify for a sabbatical an employee generally needs to have been working for the company for a specified number of years (which varies from company to company). A sabbatical is usually unpaid, but some companies do pay people, either as a reward for long service or because the sabbatical will be used to develop the employee's career in some way or it involves, say, voluntary work for a cause the company wants to support.

Traditionally, sabbaticals were a perk that academics enjoyed while the rest of the world looked on enviously. However, in the 1990s, the idea of taking a paid or unpaid break of anything between a month and a year caught on among the overstressed players of Silicon Valley and today the practice is becoming more widespread. Indeed, when IRS, an online research firm, polled 161 UK companies for its 2006 Employment Review, more than half said they would consider offering extended leave to long-serving staff. John Lewis, Tesco and Guardian Media Group are among those who offer this benefit.

It is a trend that has been driven in part by staff retention concerns, with the sabbatical providing a kind of pressure valve. And in theory at least, sabbaticals can also have a positive impact on business performance as managers return to their posts re-energised, re-enthused and ready to take a fresh look at problems.

Jonathan Denny, a managing partner at Cripps Harries Hall, a UK law firm, says sabbaticals can indeed have a beneficial effect, not only on the individuals but also on the organisations they work for. His firm is unusual in that it has operated a compulsory sabbatical policy since the 1970s. Once partners have served for ten years, they are required to clear their desks and leave the office for three months. "It's a way of rewarding partners for working hard," says Denny, "and the business justification is that it gives them a chance to recharge their batteries."

Denny went on his second sabbatical in 2011 and used the time to travel in Australia and South Africa. It was a complete break. Safe in the knowledge that he would not be contacting the office for several months, he was free to soak up the sights and reflect on his role from a healthy distance. It was time well spent, as he says:

When I returned I was asked to write a new business plan for the firm. One of the things I noticed while I was travelling was that the service ethos in Australia and South Africa was much stronger than in the UK. When I wrote my plan, I put service at the heart of our offering. The result was a new regime that rewarded partners who went the extra mile for clients.

Aiming for the top

As this book has stressed, career success has many meanings, according to people's background, values and personal circumstance. Talent is also a relative term, applying to many people who do not aspire to corporate leadership.

But if people want a conventional high-flying career with a senior management position as the goal, what personal qualities do they need other than the ones already covered in this chapter?

Ian Pearman joined Abbott Mead Vickers as a trainee in 1996, and over the years has worked on pretty much every one of the 88 brands that the advertising agency works with. He became managing partner in 2005 then managing director in 2008, and in 2010 was appointed chief executive. He highlights a number of factors that helped him reach his position.

Regular feedback

This is the first factor, as Pearman explains:

> *If you are lucky, you end up at a place where feedback is consistent and frequent but also informal. Of course most feedback in companies is done formally and infrequently. This place was good at the former rather than the latter. You get a sense of how you are doing fairly quickly in the first 12–24 months and that inevitably builds your confidence – and where the feedback is not so good you get the chance to reflect and recalibrate accordingly.*
>
> *So I had a growing sense of confidence over those early years, which further fuelled my ambition. It is a virtuous circle. Good feedback builds confidence. Confidence builds ambition and expectation, which in turn inspire great performance, which creates better feedback. These are the four components of the circle, with feedback being the first component.*

Identifying the cultural capital

The second factor is the ability to identify and buy into the cultural capital of the organisation. As Pearman says:

> There is what I call the theory of cultural capital. Everybody has a marked exterior. In organisations you can very quickly build cultural capital. There is a key or a code to every organisation, the thing that makes it tick.
>
> If you can unlock that code early on in your career, then things become a lot easier because you just understand the flow, the kind of behaviours that are appropriate and admired, what you might call the cultural tramlines.
>
> It is hard for an inexperienced person to do this, which is why I refer to it as an unknown unknown. You don't even realise that this is important until somebody tells you and that is one of the things we cover in our graduate training sessions.
>
> When we are telling them how the culture works, what behaviours will be frowned upon and which will be admired, what the tone of the place is, what the smell of the place is, they don't realise it but that is the greatest thing that we can do for them.
>
> They will learn all the more functional skill sets on the job and in the course of their training. Trying to build their understanding of the cultural capital is really important. People who "get" that this is important tend to be people with higher EQ [level of emotional intelligence].

General management theory and practice

The third factor, as already explored above, is a thorough grounding in general management theory and practice and exposure to the latest business research and ideas. Pearman describes what attending the Advanced Management Programme at Harvard Business School meant for him:

> You feel that you are in the high church of capitalism. Because of the way the course is formatted, it is a boot camp for capitalism and shareholder value. The rationale for doing it for me was exactly the same as the reason for mentoring – I wanted to know what I didn't know.

There was a set of theories and a set of practical case-study-bound experience that I wanted to access, so that I could unlock some of the codes of financial strategy. There is a lexicon to some of those concepts which, even in a business in which you are working with 40–50 business clients, you just don't come across often.

It was self-managed learning for me. It was all about the content. I wanted to be sure that I understood fully the key tenets of strategic finance.

Self-confidence, self-management and self-drive

This is the fourth factor, as Pearman puts it:

There are hygiene factors of self-management that are of course essential but it is more about the core psychological drive for recognition, for achievement or for dignity.

I think people assume that star performers just have innate talent, but a lot of the rationale for why they are good derives from quite deep-seated psychological reasons that create a higher level of commitment, emotional and in some cases physical, to the job.

They will work longer hours, they will be more focused, they will be more intense and they will engage better because they have that core drive and need. I think this is often overlooked.

Attracting the attention of senior management

The fifth factor, not stressed by Pearman but important to high-flyers, can be achieved in a number of ways, some of which have been covered in earlier chapters. One is to be given the chance to lead projects that cut across all the boundaries and disciplines of the organisation and are critical to its remit or competitiveness.

Shiseido's Hadasui project is a good example. In 1995, Shiseido, a leading Japanese cosmetics producer, launched a highly successful skin lotion called Hadasui ("bare skin"). The campaign was notable because, for the first time in its history, the company based the launch around the person who devised the new product, Norika Shimada, a 31-year-old marketing executive. This was a significant break with the company's faceless traditions, which reflected the mores of Japanese industry as a whole. In the previous two years the company had launched a series of successful products but at no point had publicly recognised the originator.

The role Shimada played in the launch is a testament to the internal struggle she underwent to get the product approved. Hadasui's main ingredient is mineral water from the slopes of Mount Fuji. At the time, there was a boom in sales of mineral water in Japan and Shimada came up with the idea for the product after using mineral water in a number of ways at home.

The marketing concept behind Hadasui – that skin should have mineral water to "drink" too – did not go down well with Shiseido's conservative senior management. They felt that the message was too "faddy" and did not fit well with the company's recent product launches. Shimada had to lobby individual board members with little or no help from colleagues in her own department. At the same time, she had to do her day-to-day work. It took nearly a year of lobbying to get the product accepted and a further two years to get it onto the market.

Shimada decided to use her own story as the centrepiece for the launch. This too was a departure from tradition. Japanese newspapers and magazines scrambled to get the story, resulting in major publicity and record sales for the product. "The launch vindicated my persistence but it was a gamble," she says. "If you stick your neck out you have to risk it might get cut off."

Shiseido's directors learnt many lessons from the Hadasui launch, the most important being that individual recognition is crucial in encouraging frontline staff to be more creative. They have since abolished the internal *sempai-kohai* relationships, where senior managers take precedence in everything and are addressed by their rank by junior staff.

Another lesson is that good ideas are often inspired outside the workplace through connections with ideas and experiences that are often unrelated to the company's sector or industry. To broaden their experience, senior managers now attend seminars where speakers discuss topics as diverse as international gymnastics and the work of Japan's volunteer medical service in developing countries.

Shimada's career moved on in leaps and bounds as a result of her leadership of the Hadasui project, but her ambitions, and those of people like her, have been helped by two other characteristics.

The first is the ability to leverage the benefits of personal sponsorship. Chapter 4 touched on the fact that the chances of women being appointed to senior posts have been boosted by sponsorship schemes, in which individuals are supported in teams or roles by a senior manager who takes personal responsibility for their advancement.

Neeha Khurana, head of learning and leadership development at Bank of America Merrill Lynch, has been particularly vocal in proclaiming the benefits of these kinds of schemes. As she commented at a talent summit in 2012:

> This kind of scheme is for our top talented women. It pairs them up with the leadership executive committee and the job of the sponsor of the leadership committee is to be an advocate, to give some exposure to these women in the right places to develop them. From my perspective, the success is really around conversations and people being open to being challenged.

The second characteristic is the personal contact rising stars have with an organisation's chief executive. Chapter 2 outlined how the chief executives of Unilever, Olam International and PepsiCo regularly met members of their talent pool. In the case of Sunny George Verghese of Olam, it is for the specific task of outlining and getting buy-in for the company's values and objectives.

Doug Baillie of Unilever describes how managers earmarked for senior positions regularly meet members of the board and the senior management team to discuss how their careers should progress and learn about the company's strategy and future direction.

Conclusion

The assumption in this chapter is that you equate "talent" with "leadership" or "getting to the top". But of course this is not the whole story. There are many people who have specialist skills and who, as Patricia Leighton describes in Chapter 6, are happy to trade work–life balance and autonomy against conventional career success by operating as independent self-employed people – a category that labour-market research suggests is growing by over 10% a year.

There are many more who are happy to let their spouse or partner take the career lead and combine job-sharing, part-time or freelance work with the responsibility of bringing up a family. And there are specialist staff who want to stay specialist and not progress to leadership roles. Some companies are responding to their needs by creating separate talent pools, to make sure that individuals wishing to progress within their own specialism are developed and remunerated as well as those with high-flying aspirations.

As Marielle de Macker, HR managing director of Randstad, comments:

> *I think we need to go in the direction of including specialists in talent planning. Typically, when people talk about talent – myself included – they mean leadership talent. But what will become more and more important will be "expert" talent. Talent with expert knowledge and expertise about their products, markets, technology, processes. The notion of "talent" will expand beyond the generalist leadership talent we all know. This will require an adjustment in our talent development structures and philosophies as well as in our remuneration and reward structures.*

People who take this holistic view of career planning may well exhibit as much "talent" as the high-flying corporate captains or the entrepreneurs but for very different personal ends. For them, being confident, being opportunistic and building the support network to achieve their own personal aspirations is just as important.

Whether they are aiming for the top, a specialist role or a more semi-detached relationship with their organisation as a consultant, contract worker or part-timer, people need to be frank with their employer about these aspirations.

As Chapter 4 demonstrated, the best employers are attempting to introduce more transparency in the way they negotiate career plans with their talented employees.

8 Planning for the future

Going forward, I think all of us need to rewrite the book on talent management ... We have the chance to look at talent in a whole new way because our people, our organisation and our shareholders are going to demand it.

Indra Nooyi, president and chief executive, PepsiCo

THE RESEARCH FOR THIS BOOK involved looking at how organisations currently "manage talent" and whether those approaches are effective and appropriate, given a less predictable business environment. The research also looked at what talented individuals actually want and respond to. The ultimate aim, which this concluding chapter seeks to do, was to come up with insights and guiding principles that can be used to manage talent as successfully as possible.

Losers and winners in the battle

This book started with a prediction made 15 years ago by McKinsey of a world where companies would be locked in a constant and costly battle for the best people – those with abilities, intrinsic gifts, skills, knowledge, experience, intelligence, judgment, attitude, character and drive that make them indispensable to their employers.

McKinsey's predictions have proved accurate. High unemployment rates among graduates make it no easier for employers to find sufficient numbers of suitably able people they would like to employ.

As Chapter 1 outlined, part of the reason is increased demand for those who can, for example, keep pace with technology, cope with uncertainty, work more collaboratively (often across national boundaries) and manage diverse teams.

Demographic trends are likely to cause substantial changes in workforces around the world. Some countries will have ageing workforces, while in others the proportion of young and relatively unskilled workers will increase. Talent planners will have to respond flexibly and imaginatively to these shifts.

High unemployment rates among young people in Western economies mean that many have got off to a slow start in their careers. Part of the problem is that the education system in many countries is failing to equip them with the right blend of knowledge and practical skills that employers want. At the same time, many of these employers are unwilling to give young adults work experience or training to help them make the transition from education to employment.

One of the effects of globalisation has been the emergence of an internationally mobile group of people who can pick and choose where they work and who are now in much demand.

The difficulties employers face are exacerbated by changes in attitudes towards work and employment. Many employees expect a better balance between work and their personal lives and want to work for a company that shares their values. A new generation of talented workers may not be willing or motivated to stay with one employer for long, whatever the financial rewards and career opportunities on offer.

Good intentions, deficient processes

The crucial importance of talented people to a business's success is beyond doubt, and many large companies have formally recognised this by establishing a talent management function.

Yet there is now a well-established body of research that reveals that many companies struggle with their talent strategies and are by no means confident that their approaches will guarantee enough leaders and specialists of the right calibre for their current and future needs.

Despite good intentions, many companies struggle to get off the starting line. Talent planning is often out of line with the business strategy, leading to a sense that HR is better at administrative tasks than working strategically to support business priorities. The big challenge for many companies is to formulate relevant notions of potential and outstanding performance in the midst of rapid business change. Operational heads need to be able to fill talent gaps as quickly as possible, yet there must also be a strategy supported by planning measures that will build the capabilities needed for longer-term business success. An organisation must have the ability to "lean into the future", and to do this managers and the HR staff who support them need to strengthen their skills in strategic planning and become more adept at identifying the HR and talent implications whenever there is a shift in business direction or the external business environment changes.

There are three main ways organisations can fulfil their need for talent: by buying it, borrowing it in the form of temporary freelancers or consultants, or building it internally through training and development of existing staff. They can also seek to widen their access to talented people, as outlined in Chapter 6.

Large international companies have tended to focus on developing their own staff to create a reliable "pipeline" of highly capable people who can fill critical positions throughout the organisation, not just senior leadership roles. It is an approach that involves joining together disparate HR processes so that they support the talent plan. However, it has potential drawbacks. The notion of a pipeline helps organisations understand where talent flows in, where it flows out and where there are blockages. This is a good starting point but a poor end point because it encourages a belief that the organisation owns and controls talent, and it can encourage a mechanistic view of talent as a commodity.

Outstanding individuals come in all shapes and sizes and organisations need to take a more customised and personalised approach if they are to keep hold of them. They can no longer dictate how and where someone works. Highly capable people tend to plan their own careers and these days often have access to career opportunities anywhere in the world. Furthermore, recruiters can find such individuals at the touch of a button.

New technology is opening up entrepreneurial opportunities to the technically savvy generation Y. Technology is also empowering talented individuals to work where and when they want to.

FIG 8.1 **Aligning business and talent strategies**

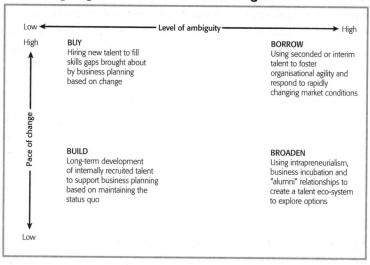

Low ◄——————— Level of ambiguity ———————► High

High

Pace of change

BUY
Hiring new talent to fill skills gaps brought about by business planning based on change

BORROW
Using seconded or interim talent to foster organisational agility and respond to rapidly changing market conditions

BUILD
Long-term development of internally recruited talent to support business planning based on maintaining the status quo

BROADEN
Using intrapreneurialism, business incubation and "alumni" relationships to create a talent eco-system to explore options

Low

Source: Marion Devine and Michel Syrett, 2013

It is crucial that organisations and individuals are honest about what they want and need. It is no longer a matter of buying and selling talent but of how the two parties broker a deal that delivers mutual but different benefits.

The way that talent management has been managed through processes and programmes has led to the function developing a life and raison d'être of its own, sucking in more and more resources and creating unnecessary bureaucracy. Talent-building processes become insulated from the external competitive environment because too much effort is spent on the operational "how" and not enough on the strategic "why".

Top managers may be tempted to abdicate their responsibility for talent management to the HR team because it is so heavily associated with programmes and procedures. And talented individuals may become invisible to top management.

The traditional talent management approach works best in a business context that is reasonably stable and where definitions of talent and potential remain meaningful and relevant long enough for career planning purposes. However, a more volatile and unpredictable environment requires a more flexible and responsive approach.

Figure 8.1 demonstrates how firms should focus on building, buying, borrowing or broadening their talent depending on their strategic context.

Low pace of change, low level of ambiguity

The business environment is relatively stable and the future predictable enough to determine strategy over the short and medium term. Firms can make accurate forecasts about the expertise critical staff need to deliver the strategy. Traditional talent management can focus on building the right combination of knowledge and experience among internal staff.

High pace of change, low level of ambiguity

This is a time of rapid change but with a clear outlook on the future. Longer-term learning and development plans are in place to help upgrade the organisation, but some critical skills are needed immediately and must be bought via external recruitment.

High pace of change, high level of ambiguity

There is no basis for forecasting the future and the priority is to anticipate and respond to unexpected events. Borrowing temporary or interim skilled staff is a way for firms to reconfigure their capabilities to explore or exploit a new opportunity. It also enables them to avoid long-term staffing decisions that would make it harder to change course should the need arise (for example, because of disruptive technology).

Low pace of change, high level of ambiguity

There is a range of possible futures and the emphasis is on scenario and contingency planning. The priority is to explore options and pick up on any cues or signals from the external environment. Through broadening their access to talented people, firms can reach beyond their boundaries, both mental and organisational, and tap into new ideas and perspectives from a diverse array of independent or creative thinkers.

New priorities

There is a widespread view among senior managers that talent planning should be strategic and integrated and much less tactical and piecemeal. Asked about the challenges that "keep them awake at night", those interviewed for this book identified a range of issues that can be grouped into four segments.

One big concern is how to align talent management with the overall strategy so that it can respond to the (often urgent) needs of the business. The other three concerns flow from this: how to redefine talent and potential in the light of strategic priorities; how to deploy talented people across the business for maximum impact; and how to create a corporate culture where a wider and more diverse group of talented individuals can thrive.

Alignment

The organisations and leaders featured in this book are grappling with how to design talent strategies and processes in the context of highly uncertain yet fast-changing business environments.

As the example of Unilever in Chapter 2 highlights, success in global markets depends on seizing opportunities and moving into new competitive areas. The company has ambitious growth plans and is expanding fast into new activities.

This means that business planning must be done in shorter cycles and companies must be more flexible, using scenario and contingency planning in case the strategy needs to change suddenly. They cannot afford a lengthy interval between strategy formulation and implementation and must have people in place who can manage changes in direction or emphasis.

The research and interviews carried out for this book revealed the need for organisations to:

- make sure that their talent strategy keeps pace with growth targets, so that they are able to fill new roles as they arise rather than playing catch-up by "back-filling";
- create global talent pools and ensure that a small cluster of nationalities do not dominate;

- respond rapidly to a shift of business activity towards growing or emerging markets – for example, make sure that managers from these regions are included in the talent pool and that career planning includes work assignments in these markets;
- quickly plug skills gaps and amend learning and development plans when the business changes direction and needs a new set of capabilities to deliver the strategy;
- remain aligned with business strategy – the top management team and senior managers need to collaborate more effectively with those in HR to make sure that talent management stays tightly focused on business needs.

Redefining who and what constitutes talent

As the examples of Olam International, Mars, Santander UK and Randstad revealed, a big issue is how to define talent and potential in the light of business priorities.

Many companies have been defining what they mean by outstanding performance and are re-evaluating what is the optimum mix of general management skills and specialist expertise. They now need to:

- distinguish outstanding leadership from merely good leadership and make sure that talent strategies focus on the latter;
- define talent and potential in terms that reflect the context of the business as well as its values, and which remain relevant despite changes in the business strategy or organisation structure;
- move away from a homogeneous senior leadership team towards a more diverse pool of talent – not just in terms of culture, ethnicity, gender and age, but also in terms of thinking and attitude, background and experience;
- attract digitally savvy employees who are creative and innovative – and create an organisational environment where they can thrive;
- find the right ratio between internal and external appointments – for some companies the priority is to inject "new blood" into senior management teams, while for others growing their

own is important to ensure a continuity of cultural values and behaviours;

■ understand the personal attributes needed so that someone's talent can be developed and harnessed for maximum value – and consider whether critical traits such as ability to learn, self-awareness, resilience and adaptability can be taught or developed.

Deploying talent

The priority is to have the right array of talented people in the right places in the organisation equipped with the right skills and experiences to execute the strategy. Organisations need to:

■ keep hold of talented young employees long enough for them to be included in talent management plans – an urgent concern is how to manage their expectations and avoid over-accelerating their careers so they consolidate their skills;

■ improve the progression of talented women into senior and top management positions;

■ develop managers and specialists who can help create new business models and also work across a range of business models at different stages of their careers;

■ accelerate the development and career progression of some employees, especially when there is an urgent need to plug a skills gap, or expand the pool of talent to include an underutilised group of talented people;

■ identify high-potential individuals early enough so that they can be given the right experiences and development opportunities.

Building a culture to attract, recognise and develop talent

A concern about building a genuine rather than "painted-on" talent-based culture has moved from "nice to have" to a major preoccupation among those interviewed for this book. Indeed, some believe that having the right culture is more important than having well-designed formal talent processes. In general, the desire is to create a culture that:

- gets the best out of people and encourages them to take risks and stretch themselves to reach their full potential;
- ensures the business is seen as the "employer of choice" among its target group of talented individuals;
- is perceived as authentic, where cultural values are consistently applied, even when the business experiences challenges and setbacks;
- remains undiluted and cohesive during phases of change such as rapid business growth;
- encourages senior managers to nurture talented individuals.

The individual perspective

Organisations know what they need from their employees, but where do talented individuals fit in? What do they want from their careers and what is their experience of being "talent managed"?

What is clear is that the kind of people who are so much in demand these days want:

- to feel valued and respected;
- competitive salaries;
- rapid job advancement;
- a sense of achievement;
- exciting and challenging work;
- freedom and autonomy;
- a good work–life balance.

Moreover, many have expectations and attitudes that traditional talent management strategies do not really allow for.

Talented people are not like chess pieces that can be moved at the whim of the organisation. They are ambitious, demanding, often impatient, and intolerant of boredom, hierarchy and politics. They know their value and are willing to move jobs and companies to get what they want. They want opportunities to develop their skills, but they may not want to play the talent game for the following reasons:

- They have an individualistic approach to career planning – they believe they own their talent and they expect to manage their own career.

- They do not automatically want a long-term corporate career – they are well aware of other employment opportunities available to them such as self-employment or working for a charity or a non-governmental organisation.

- They do not automatically want to be included in a talent pool or to be given the label of "talented".

- They do not want to sacrifice everything to get to the top – and they are often unwilling to be mobile at certain stages of life.

- They think more flexibly about life stages and are more willing than ever before to move jobs frequently, embark on career changes and have spells without employment to concentrate on family commitments or pursue more qualifications.

- They have a degree of scepticism, even cynicism, about whether companies live up to their espoused values.

- They do not easily give their loyalty to a company – this has to be earned.

Not so strategically talented

Overall, the research for this book suggests a fundamental misalignment between the attitudes and expectations of organisations and talented individuals. The strategies many organisations have adopted with regard to making sure that their need for talent is met are in trouble for the following reasons:

- International companies are putting emphasis in the early identification of talent and long-term career planning in the face of increasing numbers of talented individuals who do not have the patience or inclination to commit to a lengthy career with one organisation.

- There is a failure to accommodate the desires and needs of the innovative and creative individuals, such as entrepreneurs and mavericks, who can help organisations adapt and stay ahead in a volatile business environment.

- For personal reasons and commitments, many talented people are less willing to move around when international companies need or would like them to.

- Talented women are being held back or because of corporate inflexibility are leaving large organisations, thus making it even less likely that they will build the more diverse leadership teams they need.

- A focus on succession planning implicitly equates "talent" with the "top", just at a time when talented people seem more thoughtful about their careers and less certain about what constitutes high achievement.

- A focus on the "core" of firm-specific workers and managers, often in full-time posts, ignores the fact that many people with these core skills are electing to work at the periphery of the organisation in part-time, contract and associate roles.

- An assumption that talent retention means retaining valued staff in continuous, permanent employment inside the organisation fails to recognise that many talented people now think in terms of a more varied "portfolio" career.

A new model

The solution to the strategic disconnect with reality is a closer convergence between business agendas and the life and career goals of high-flying individuals, and to build pools of talent not just from within the organisation but also from the periphery and outside the business altogether.

This more flexible and inclusive approach to talent management is illustrated in Figure 8.2, which shows different approaches to managing diverse talent pools.

Traditional talent management focuses on the top and bottom left quadrants, where the aim is to recruit talent into the organisation. In broad terms, programme-led approaches are used with large talent pools and for younger talent. As the pipeline narrows and talented individuals become increasing skilled and more valuable, the emphasis is on more tailored approaches. The goal is to retain the

FIG 8.2 **Managing diverse talent pools**

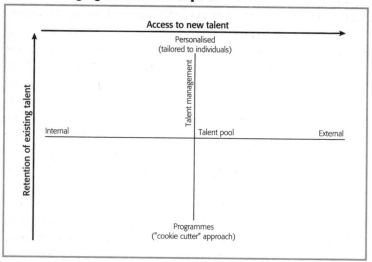

Source: Marion Devine and Michel Syrett, 2013

talent and make sure that both the individual and the organisation are getting what they want.

However, this traditional approach means that young employees and more junior women are often in the bottom left quadrant when they should be in the top left quadrant because of their propensity to leave the organisation when they are not getting the opportunities they want.

A more innovative approach is to "stretch" the talent strategy into all four quadrants – to connect with those who have been overlooked or who have opted out because their needs have not been accommodated, and to forge relationships with people outside the organisation who have the desired skills, ideas, knowledge, experience and networks.

Internal talent

Instead of being exclusively geared to getting a small number of employees to the top of the business, the internal strategy needs to focus on making sure that talented people at all levels of the business are deployed for maximum effect – even when an individual does not want to move to the next level, or when there is limited opportunity for promotion. This means that as much attention should be given to high-performing specialists or those employees who occupy critical roles but are not likely to progress further as to the next generation of top leaders.

The talent strategy needs to be designed from the outset to accommodate a broader pool of talent. Close attention should be paid to the needs of women and young employees to make sure that they are given the right work experiences and development opportunities at a time that suits their career aspirations and personal circumstances.

Mavericks and intrapreneurs also need special attention and this may require inventive ways to be found, as discussed in Chapter 6, to build more conducive work environments that will help retain these individuals and give their innovative and creative gifts free rein.

The aim must be to create a compelling employee value proposition supported by a set of values and behaviours to make sure that talented people feel respected and valued and that the people responsible for them are keeping an eye on their development and career progression.

The management of diverse talent pools can range from a programme-led approach, through to more tailored and personalised intervention.

In the bottom left quadrant, a programme-led approach works well when large numbers of talented individuals have similar needs. For example, graduate training programmes are an effective way to begin equipping individuals for a career in an organisation. Other programmes might include learning and development programmes or qualification-based skills training.

However, at some point it may be appropriate to operate in the top left quadrant by taking a more tailored and personal approach to a specific employee or group of employees. This could be for a variety of reasons: there is a strong risk they will leave; they are critical for a current or future role or project; they have a rare talent that would be difficult to replace; there are long-term plans to develop them.

Companies must understand what motivates these high-flying

individuals and what they want, and then seek to "broker" an agreement that gets the best and most out of them while satisfying their needs and desires. This requires openness on both sides and highly flexible career planning.

The majority of the companies featured in this book are adopting more tailored approaches to talent management. Olam International, for example, may depend on a programme-led approach to help process the large number of managers that have been recruited, but it relies on its culture to make sure that these managers connect with the values of the business, and the chief executive makes a point of personally meeting new members of the talent pool.

PepsiCo is positioned at the top of the vertical axis because of its move towards "intelligent profiling" as a means of career planning and its aim to "bond" talent by forging strong personal relationships between the top management team and the people in the pool for the company's 300 critical positions.

The task for organisations that are adopting more tailored and personalised approaches is no longer to "manage" talent but to keep talented individuals fulfilled and feeling valued – the more they feel as though they in a talent pool of "one" the more likely that is.

Peripheral and external talent

By moving across to the top and bottom right quadrants, organisations can build a talent "ecosystem". The goal is to tap into the talents not only of employees at the core of the organisation but also of those at the periphery, in satellite organisations (such as a joint venture or a valued supplier) and outside the organisation (such as specialist freelancers and independent consultants).

Instead of straining to keep talent "captive" at all costs, the emphasis is on maintaining a relationship with past and potential future employees. This means accepting that it is not always possible, or indeed desirable, to retain every talented employee. Companies maintain relationships with former employees for various reasons, such as business development or marketing, but this can be integrated into the talent strategy.

A programme-led approach in the bottom right quadrant is

appropriate when a company wants to create linkages with specific groups of talented people. Talent management managers may have ownership of such programmes or liaise with the sections of the business that oversee these activities, such as Santander UK's internship programme and Telefónica's business incubation programme run through its Wayra Academy (see Chapter 6).

Changing direction

Overall, companies might choose to move towards the top left quadrant when they need to retain their talented people or want their most talented staff to commit to long-term career plans, which might include international assignments, as in the case of Mars and Unilever. Another reason for moving in this direction is when a programme-based approach is not meeting the needs of specific individuals or groups.

Companies might opt for the bottom left quadrant and a more programme-based approach when they feel the need for more consistency. For example, some of those interviewed for this book were concerned that judgments about talent and potential were made inconsistently across the business, with too much emphasis on intuition and not enough on objective assessment.

Other reasons for moving down to the bottom left quadrant might be because a company has grown so rapidly that its talent management has become piecemeal and ad hoc. Moving towards a programme-based approach helps create more consistency and makes it easier for the company to ensure that talent activities are co-ordinated in a coherent strategy.

A move towards the bottom right quadrant can be the best way to tap into the talent of large groups. Gulf International Bank, for example, has used co-creation with customers to help it design some of the features of its new retail business. Companies such as Google use crowd sourcing and other forms of "mass collaboration" to gain access to new ideas.

Other programme-led approaches include efforts to fill serious skills gaps, for example in science and technology. This might involve working with government bodies and educational establishments to attract more students into these areas or into related careers.

Movement towards the top right quadrant is determined by a scarcity of talent or the need to access new talent that is not available within the organisation.

Companies that are moving in this direction often do so when they need to tap into rare talent or are looking for exceptionally innovative and creative individuals. In this case, such individuals are carefully tracked and the organisation looks for every opportunity to cultivate a relationship with them.

Companies might also move towards the right side of the model when they lack the ability to develop the required talent internally and it is not realistic to try to recruit. For instance, PepsiCo has all but given up trying to recruit people with digital skills. Richard Evans, president of PepsiCo UK, Ireland and South Africa, admits:

> We've taken people from Google, we've taken people from eBay and the reality is that they haven't stayed very long ... They are in a digital space because they love the digital environment. We do not have the same culture ... Our learning is that we have to think of another model here.

Tapping into a bigger and more diverse pool of talent can also improve an organisation's adaptive ability. If it can create more flexible and responsive relationships with talented people and sources of talent both within and outside the organisation, it is better positioned to engineer a change in strategic direction.

The model for managing diverse talent pools can also be used as a diagnostic tool to assess whether the chosen mode for managing a specific talent pool is no longer producing the required talent output for the business strategy.

An example is Cisco Systems, a multinational technology company. Back in the early 1990s, its talent strategy concentrated on aggressively acquiring external talent, either through massive recruitment programmes for hardware and software engineers or by buying smaller players in the industry. As part of a turnaround effort in 2001, Cisco changed its strategy from aiming to recruit the best engineers to focusing on its internal talent. It wanted to help these individuals move out of strictly delineated knowledge areas and become more versatile. The goal was to produce a pool of adaptable employees who thrived on change and could move quickly into different areas of the business, or who could "mix" their skills into new combinations in response to external change.

Through Cisco University, the company's centre for learning and development, employees gained access to personalised career planning and tailored e-learning. They could also post their experiences and career aspirations on various internal websites, and company managers were actively encouraged to try to move people into different work assignments or jobs.

In terms of the talent pool model, Cisco moved swiftly from the bottom left quadrant, where it focused on recruiting large groups of engineers, to the top left quadrant, where it focused on internal talent and a more tailored approach to career planning and learning and development.

Its former approach no longer served the needs of the business. For a time, having the best engineers enabled Cisco to become an industry leader. However, as the technology boom ended, Cisco had to reconfigure its business to become more adaptable and innovative. The talent strategy had to shift, and the way the company managed its internal talent pool also had to change.

Moving up the value chain

The traditional approach to talent management can lead to a plethora of programmes and initiatives and a machine that develops a life of its own, blind to what it is there to achieve. An ecosystem model encourages a more strategic approach in its concentration on the top left and right quadrants.

In the left space, more tailored and personalised approaches need to be brokered by talent managers who have a strategic overview and a keen understanding of the opportunities available to talented individuals across different functions, business units and geographies.

In the right quadrant, relationships with external talent in whatever guise also need to be managed by those who understand the business strategy, how this may evolve in the future, and how the business can benefit from these external relationships immediately or at some stage in the future.

Similarly, it can be argued that talent managers who spend most or all of their time overseeing programme-led approaches are contributing relatively less value to the organisation and should consider moving towards the top quadrants of the model.

New principles

In conclusion, here are eight guiding principles for managing talent in a more volatile and uncertain world, where talent is in demand and talented people have more power and discretion over how they contribute their talent to an organisation:

- **A deep and genuine commitment to deploy talent for maximum business impact.** Both managers and staff recognise that seeding the brightest people across the organisation will have a tangible impact on business performance. Finding and nurturing these high-flyers is everyone's responsibility, not just that of senior managers or HR. The quality and quantity of talent within an organisation marks it out from its rivals and gives it a vital competitive edge.

- **A talent plan goes hand-in-hand with the design and execution of the business strategy.** The senior executive team is regularly consulted and briefed by the talent director to make sure that the talent strategy is aligned with business needs. Changes in business strategy are swiftly factored into the talent model. The alignment of business and talent strategies helps create a talent management strategy that is agile and is capable of responding to changes in the competitive landscape.

- **Talented individuals are partners, not pawns, in any process to harness their abilities.** The talent strategy is driven by a broader definition of talent so that the organisation benefits from the gifts of a diverse array of individuals, including those from underrepresented groups of employees. Talent planners recognise that the organisation does not own talented individuals and that they can choose whether they bring all their energy, skill and creativity to work. Talent planning is done in a spirit of openness and collaboration, not secrecy or control.

■ **A culture that fosters talent is the bedrock of a successful talent strategy.** The management of culture is a major part of the talent strategy. A talent-based culture acts like a magnet to attract high-flyers and helps create an environment where they can thrive. Bright people outside the organisation are attracted by its values and purpose. The chief executive and senior management uphold the values underpinning the culture. Talented people feel respected and valued. Mentoring, coaching and sponsorship allow senior managers to get to know gifted individuals and take an active role in their development.

■ **A successful talent strategy stands or falls on the direct involvement of the chief executive.** The active sponsorship of the chief executive emphasises the organisation's commitment to developing talent and helps to "bond" the senior management team to its values and remit.

■ **Talent managers have close links with business heads and the senior executive team and work at a strategic level to achieve the business plan.** The task is handled by a talent management function, with a head of talent who is accountable to the chief executive. Talent heads are skilled in strategic planning and workforce planning.

■ **Talent pools of many should feel like a pool of one.** There is open communication between talented individuals and talent managers about how personal aspirations can be matched with business needs. Career planning is tailored and personal. The aim is not to manage talent but to keep talented people fulfilled.

■ **The talent strategy helps build an ecosystem that extends beyond the borders of the organisation.** The talent ecosystem helps the organisation tap into the talent that currently resides outside the business. Organisational boundaries no longer matter, and employees at the core and periphery are all included in the talent strategy. Relationship takes precedence over employment. The values that underpin the organisation are extended across the ecosystem, as are development opportunities, with a strong emphasis on shared learning.

Executive summary

1 The war for talent: talent management to the rescue?

Traditional talent management assumes that high-flying employees want to get to the top of the pile and will do whatever their organisations require to get there. However, a new generation of talented workers may not be willing or motivated to stay with one employer for long, whatever the financial rewards and career opportunities on offer. This makes long-term career planning much more difficult for organisations.

In this respect:

- The struggle for the best staff has broadened beyond senior leadership talent. There is intense competition among employers for highly skilled people for a wide variety of managerial and specialist positions.

- An increasing number of talented people who are internationally mobile can pick and choose where they work – and are now in demand by firms operating in emerging markets.

- American and European firms are experiencing serious skills shortages, despite continued high unemployment in many industries. The main obstacle is the lack of people with the right degree of experience, skills or knowledge to fill these positions, indicating a widespread failure of countries to produce enough people with the level of education and skills that employers need to remain competitive.

- As business and jobs have become more complex, firms increasingly look for individuals with a range of abilities and experience that might include technological or other specialist skills, broader functional skills, industry expertise and knowledge of specific geographical markets.

■ The established approach to talent management is beginning to look outmoded and ineffective in the face of the demand for talent and the demands and desires of talented individuals. Talent management needs to become more flexible and to involve a more diverse range of people both within and outside the organisation if it is to enable a business to change direction as circumstances demand.

2 Devising and implementing a talent strategy

Talent planning must be led by a company's strategic goals and priorities and should be based on a rigorous assessment of its short- and medium-term talent requirements. This can be done effectively only if there is the active involvement and support of the executive team, operational heads and other senior managers. It also requires that those in HR have greater expertise than is often the case in strategic workforce planning and other strategic planning processes such as scenario planning.

The greatest risk and the greatest irony are that in an effort to become more rigorous and systematic at talent management, organisations may end up building systems that are too rigid for today's more turbulent conditions.

In this respect:

■ Developing and implementing the organisation's talent strategy should go hand-in-hand with the design and execution of the business strategy, to avoid a misalignment between the needs of the business and the output of succession planning.

■ The task should be handled by a specific (and often global) talent management function. The head of talent should be accountable directly to the chief executive rather than the head of HR – yet a study by Heidrick & Struggles in 2010 suggests that this rarely occurs.

- The senior executive team should be regularly consulted and briefed by the global talent director so that:
  - talent strategy is aligned with the business strategy and can deliver in the long term through regular conversations and reviews;
  - any changes in business strategy are factored into the talent model adopted by the organisation as quickly as possible;
  - the talent management strategy is agile and capable of responding to any change in the competitive landscape.
  - The direct involvement of the chief executive is crucial to emphasise the importance of the function and make sure that it is properly aligned with the business strategy. Also critical is the involvement of operational heads across the company to make sure that people with the right skills and experience are recruited to the top management team.

3 Managing the talent process

In the past decade there has been growing use of a process-led approach to talent planning which has focused on a small cohort of high-flyers who are destined to become future top leaders. Such an approach works well when the business environment is relatively stable and companies are reasonably confident about their strategies and the capabilities to execute their plans successfully.

A process-based "machine" helps ensure consistency and a useful end-to-end view of how and where talent needs to enter and move across the organisation. The drawback is that it becomes unwieldy. It becomes so resource intensive that its focus and energies are directed at what it does rather than what it is meant to achieve in terms of supporting the business strategy.

Companies in uncertain or highly competitive conditions are rethinking their approach to talent management. They are not necessarily dismantling their systems but are looking at the question of how to build more flexibility.

In this respect:

- Companies should avoid building an overly complex "talent machine" and must constantly ask themselves whether what they are doing in terms of talent management is achieving the desired results.

- In complex and fast-changing conditions, the talent strategy needs to be more flexible so that the right capabilities are ready for deployment when and where they are needed.

- A broader definition of talent will allow companies to draw on diverse sources of talent, notably women, who might otherwise be overlooked by traditional processes. Companies have to define the leadership and technical abilities that most suit their business contexts. It is also important to make sure that their talented staff can work equally effectively in different business models and can cope with uncertainty and pressure.

- Some companies are placing greater importance on finding the right people rather than the right skills. Skills can be learnt, but traits such as commitment or energy cannot.

- Talent needs to be increasingly mobile, but companies need greater skills in strategic workforce planning to ensure they plug their skills gaps and develop their talented staff. This also requires companies to make sure that their talent is visible to the whole organisation.

- Career planning should keep in mind the long view and be more personal and customised, taking into account individual characteristics and circumstances; for example, when considering international assignments.

4 The individual and the organisation

Increasing numbers of employees, not just women and young employees, are taking an individualistic approach to their careers and may not be willing to sacrifice everything to get to the top. Talented individuals appear much less loyal to their organisations. They are strongly committed to developing their own talent and pursuing their own goals before those of the organisation.

Organisations need to take on board this new reality and offer the right development opportunities and work experiences – otherwise talented people will leave.

Flexible career planning can help satisfy talented people, but it may not be sufficient to gain their trust and loyalty. Despite the best processes, some talented individuals continue to enter companies, learn what they can and then move on – throwing succession plans into disarray.

In this respect:

- People from generation Y (broadly, those born between 1980 and 2000) pose challenges for talent management. It is a generation with high expectations and a low tolerance level, voting with its feet if employers fail to deliver.

- Graduates' expectations of a rapid rise to management may be unrealistic but still pose difficulties for organisations that do not want to lose genuinely talented people; high-flying women and older high-performing individuals share many of the frustrations of ambitious talented graduates.

- Four dimensions of work are crucial for motivating and retaining talented individuals: rapid job advancement; money and challenging work; work–life balance; and freedom and autonomy.

- In concert with the five dimensions there must be a compelling "employee value proposition", which entails offering each talented individual the right set of career inducements.

- Career planning must be highly tailored and personal for the segment of talented employees whose contribution is crucial to the longer-term strategy.

- Flexible career planning has six dimensions: open and honest career discussions; personalised career opportunities; frequent career reviews; career trellises (which allow people to further their careers while making sideways moves and pursuing specialist avenues); flexible working arrangements; tailored learning and development and the use of coaches, mentors and sponsors.

5 Taking a culture-led approach

If companies want to recruit and retain the best-performing employees, they need to espouse values and goals that will encourage an emotional commitment to and personal identification with the organisation.

Senior leaders play a crucial role in "bonding" talent to the organisation by making time to get to know these individuals and showing how much the company values their contribution. A culture that engages employees and helps give meaning to their work will help keep them loyal to the company even when the going gets tough.

However, companies that become obsessed with achieving a tight cultural "fit" between the organisation and the individual can become unduly risk adverse in their recruitment and selection decisions, with the result that they forgo the chance to take on those such as creative or entrepreneurially minded individuals who are different but have a lot to offer.

In this respect:

- There must be a compelling rationale for why anyone should work for an organisation.
- The values and cultural mores of an organisation must be "lived" and followed by the chief executive and the senior management team and applied consistently.
- These values must be reflected in the way top talent is developed, providing "disruptive" learning opportunities through secondments and assignments that promote and reflect the organisation's commitment to the communities in which it operates.
- Ideally, an organisation should be transparent about employees' prospects, boosting their confidence and commitment and taking each individual's desires and circumstances into account in developing their capabilities and career planning.

6 Creating a talent eco-structure

Developing a talent "ecosystem" helps overcome the problems of in-house dependence in a world where talented people are less likely to commit to long-term employment in an organisation. What used to be termed "the periphery" consisting of those who choose to work part time or be self-employed is growing.

There is also a growing proportion of young people who are opting out of corporate employment altogether, and who have entrepreneurial skills and aspirations that large organisations have been poor at accommodating but which they need if they are to anticipate and respond effectively to unexpected change and volatility.

The use of business incubation schemes and linked-in internships, career planning specifically targeted at intrapreneurs, and relationships with former employees based on the concept of alumni and associate status enables organisations to extend their talent ecosystem. They can reach and retain talent they would otherwise lose.

However, for a talent ecosystem to work, organisations need to reach beyond their traditional boundaries.

In this respect:

■ Business incubation schemes, internships and alumni or associate relationships need to be integrated into the existing talent management strategy, opening up a two-way avenue of opportunities for corporate employees and those employed in more oblique ways.

■ Career planning should be adapted accordingly, allowing talented workers who do not want traditional corporate careers the chance to pursue entrepreneurial activities while remaining in the organisation's orbit, and alumni and associates the opportunity to return to the corporate fold if their circumstances or aspirations change.

■ The "ecosystem" of talent and the organisation should share the same core values, and cultural bonds should be strengthened through invitations to the organisation's events and social functions.

■ Those within the ecosystem should also be given or be able to take advantage of the development opportunities available to talented in-house employees.

7 Playing the talent game

For individuals who want to make the most of the opportunities their talent affords them, the three principal options are corporate management, consultancy, and setting up and running their own business. For many people who have specialist skills there is another option, operating as an independent self-employed "freelancer", a category that labour-market research suggests is growing by over 10% a year.

There are also highly specialist individuals who want to stay specialist and not progress to leadership roles. Some companies are responding to their needs by creating separate talent pools so that those wishing to progress within their own specialism are developed and rewarded on a par with those who aspire to climb the corporate ladder.

In general, what matters for anyone who wants to get on is being confident, being opportunistic and building a support network that allows personal as well as career aspirations, which may be linked, to be achieved.

It is also important that there is an open discussion between individuals and their employers about these aspirations. This applies to freelancers as well as to those on the payroll.

Interviews carried out for this book revealed several characteristics of successful people:

- They have the ability to make the company grade by achieving performance targets and demonstrating senior management potential through, for example, managing teams and projects, collaborating across disciplines, and leading with vision and inspiration.

- They are opportunistic and take risks. They do not follow a rigid career path but take advantage of openings and unexpected job offers, while retaining a longer-term vision of where they want to end up.

- They develop their own network of support, building a cadre of experienced and insightful personal contacts who can advise on career moves and difficult career issues.

- They expect to be mobile and are open with the organisation when their personal and family circumstances enable them to be so – and when they do not.

- If they are recruited to senior operational positions, they should have a thorough grounding in general management theory and practice and exposure to new ideas and research. This can be acquired either through self-sponsored study for an MBA or a related masters' qualification or through a company-sponsored management programme. Self-sponsored MBAs allow individuals to reflect on career options and provide openings to, for example, a career in management consultancy or starting up their own business.

- They have self-confidence and self-drive, fostered by regular feedback and mentoring support.

- If they are aiming for a senior management position, they identify closely with the values and remit of the organisation and understand its underlying culture and what makes it tick. They also have the ability to engage with senior executives.

8 Planning for the future

There are eight guiding principles for managing talent in a more volatile and uncertain world, where talent is in demand and talented people have more power and discretion over how they contribute their talent to an organisation:

- A deep and genuine commitment to deploy talent for maximum business impact.

- A talent plan goes hand-in-hand with the design and execution of the business strategy.

- Talented individuals are partners, not pawns, in any process to harness their abilities.

- A culture that fosters talent is the bedrock of a successful talent strategy.

- A successful talent strategy stands or falls on the direct involvement of the chief executive.

- Talent managers have close links with business heads and the senior executive team and work at a strategic level to achieve the business plan.

- Talent pools of many should feel like a pool of one.
- The talent strategy helps build an ecosystem that extends beyond the borders of the organisation.

These are explained in more detail in the last section of Chapter 8.

Acknowledgements

In producing this book, we have been helped by a number of individuals and organisations that require acknowledgement.

First, we would like to thank the Economist Conference Unit for allowing us to access and quote extracts from the presentations made at the Economist Talent Management Summits in June 2011 and 2012. This proved a mine of insights, observations and good practice.

We would like to acknowledge the support and encouragement of "thought leaders" on this topic, most notable Emily Lawson of McKinsey, David Smith of Accenture, Jean-Michel Caye and Roselinde Torres of Boston Consulting Group, Eric Olsen of Heidrick & Struggles, Paul Levett of SHL, Patricia Leighton, and Angela Baron, formerly of the UK Chartered Institute of Personnel and Development, all of whom contributed their thoughts and insights to this book.

We would also like to thank the many senior executives responsible for talent management who allowed us to interview them for the book. These include Becky Snow, global talent director at Mars Incorporated; Joydeep Bose, president and global head of human resources at Olam International, and his colleagues Janaky Grant, head of learning and development and HR business partner, and Steve Driver, head of manufacturing and technical services; Marielle de Macker, managing director of group HR at Randstad; Cornel Fourie, former chief human resources officer at Gulf International Bank; and Caroline Curtis, head of talent, performance and leadership development at Santander UK.

Then there are the "high-fliers" themselves, people with a track record of success that allowed us to capture their thoughts about being talented and being talent-managed. These include Tim Levine, who gave up a traditional corporate career to pursue a life as an entrepreneur in his 20s and is now a managing partner and founder of Augmentum Capital; Stephen Dury, director of strategy and market development at Santander UK; Ross Hall, formerly a senior manager at both GlaxoSmithKline and Pearson and now an independent entrepreneur; Simon Devonshire, London manager of the Wayra Academy, founded by Telefónica; Rajeeb Dey, entrepreneur and founder of Enternships; Rain Newton Smith, head of emerging markets at Oxford Economics; Ian Pearman, CEO of Abbott Mead Vickers; and MBA alumni Salini Joseph, Sanjar Ibragimov and Carlos Velasco. Finally, acknowledgements to Julia Irrgang and Sandra Schwarzer of INSEAD, Claire Lecoq of IMD and Fiona Sandford of London Business School for all their help.

On the editorial side, thanks to Stephen Brough and Penny Williams. Lastly, we would like to thank our partners Stephen and Suzy, for putting up with long weekends of us being chained to the computer and immersed in mutual deliberation.

Research acknowledgements

This book would not have been possible without the help of the following companies that helped with the research and the people who gave up their time to be interviewed.

Abbott Mead Vickers, advertising agency	Ian Pearman, chief executive
Accenture, management consultancy	David Smith, senior managing director
Ashridge Business School, UK-based international business school	Carina Paine Schofield, research fellow Sue Honore, independent learning consultant and project manager
AT&T, multinational telecommunications corporation	Carrie Corbin, associate director of talent acquisition
Augmentum Capital, UK private equity firm	Tim Levine, founder and partner
Boeing, global aerospace company	
Boston Consulting Group, global management consulting firm	Jean-Michel Caye, BCG Fellow and head of the HR/people advantages and talent topics for BCG globally Roselinde Torres, senior partner and managing director
BraveNewTalent.com, online social recruitment network	Lucian Tarnowski, founder and chief executive
Enternships.com, online company that finds places in SMEs for university graduates with entrepreneurial ambitions	Rajeeb Dey, founder and chief executive

Frontier Communications, American telephone company	Maggie Wilderotter, chairman and chief executive
Getty Images, company that creates and distributes images, footage and music online	Lisa Calvert, senior vice-president, human resources and facilities
Google, multinational corporation specialising in internet-related services and products	Liane Hornsey, vice-president of people operations
Gulf International Bank, based in Bahrain	Cornel Fourie, former chief human resources officer
Hays, UK recruitment company	James Cullens, group human resources director
Heidrich & Struggles, international executive search firm	Eric Olson, global managing partner of leadership consulting
IBM, multinational technology and consulting corporation	Robin Willner, former vice-president, global community initiatives
IMD, international business school based in Switzerland	Claire Lecoq, director of MBA admissions Michael Stanford, executive director
Independent consultant	Ross Hall, former director and vice-president of education for economic and social development at Pearson, multinational publishing and education company
INSEAD, international business school based in France	Sandra Schwarzer, director of career services
London Business School	Fiona Sandford, executive director, global business and careers
Mars, chocolate, confectionery and beverage conglomerate	Becky Snow, global talent director
McKinsey & Company, global management consulting firm	Emily Lawson, head of global human capital practice
Merck, global pharmaceutical company	Chris Benko, vice-president of global talent management
Naukri.com, Indian online recruitment company	Sanjeev Bikhchandani, co-founder and chief executive Hitesh Oberoi, chief operating officer

Olam International, global integrated supply chain manager and processor of agricultural products and food ingredients

Joydeep Bose, president and global head of human resources
Steve Driver, head of manufacturing and technical services
Janaky Grant, HR partner
Sunny Verghese, chief executive

Oxford Economics, global forecasting and analysis company

Rain Newton-Smith, head of emerging markets,

PepsiCo, multinational food and beverage corporation

Indra Nooyi, chairman and CEO
Richard Evans, president, PepsiCo UK, Ireland and South Africa

Procter & Gamble (P&G), multinational consumer goods company

Sonali Roychowdhury, head of HR

Randstad, multinational human-resources consulting firm

Mark Bull, UK CEO
Marielle de Macker, HR managing director

Relume, research and advisory firm

Khurshed Dehnugara, partner

Santander UK

Stephen Dury, managing director of strategy and market development
Caroline Curtis, head of talent, succession and leadership development

Tata Chemicals, global company based in India

Budaraju Sudhakar, chief human resources officer

Unilever, multinational consumer goods company

Doug Baillie, president of Unilever Western Europe and member of executive committee

University of Glamorgan, based in Scotland

Patricia Leighton, emeritus professor of employment

Wells Fargo, multinational banking and financial services company

Sources

1 The war for talent: talent management to the rescue

The Age and Employment Network, *Survey of Job Seekers 50+,* 2013

Cappelli, P., *Why Good People Cannot Get Jobs: The Skills Gap and What Companies Can Do About It,* Wharton Digital Press, 2012

Cerna, L., *Policies and practices of highly skilled migration in times of the economic crisis,* International Migration Programme, International Migration Papers, No. 99, April 2010

Chartered Institute of Professional Development, *Learning and Training Development Report,* 2011

Chartered Institute of Professional Development/Hays, *Resourcing and Talent Planning,* Annual Survey, 2013

Davidson, A., "Skills don't pay the bill", *New York Times,* November 20th 2012

Deloitte and the Manufacturing Institute, *Boiling point?: The skills gap in US manufacturing,* a report on talent in the manufacturing industry, 2011

European Centre for the Development of Vocational Training, *Future skills supply and demand in Europe: Forecast 2012,* Research Paper No. 26

European Union, *European Demography Report,* 2010

Hornsey, L., presentation at *The Economist* Talent Management Summit, June 14th 2012

International Institute for Labour Studies, *Making Migration a Development Factor,* ILO, Geneva, 2010

International Labour Organisation, *Global Employment Trends,* Geneva, 2008

ManpowerGroup, *Annual Talent Shortage Survey,* 2013

McKinsey Global Institute, *The World at Work: Jobs, Pay and Skills for 3.5 Billion People,* June 2012

Michaels, E., Handfield-Jones, H. and Axelrod, B., *The War for Talent,* Harvard Business School Press, 2001

National Employment Law Projects 2012

Oxford Economics, *Global Talent 2021: How the new geographies of talent will transform human resource strategies,* 2012

Pew Research Center, *Millennials: a Portrait of Generation Next*, February 2010

Sharmila, D., "The hiring process goes on ... and on", www.ft.com, May 8th 2013

"Working age shift: generations will suffer as workers dwindle", *The Economist*, January 26th 2013

World Economic Forum, *Stimulating Economies Through Fostering Talent Mobility*, March 2010

2 Devising and implementing a talent strategy

Accenture/IAOP (International Association of Outsourcing Professionals), "Outsourcing being used more strategically for higher knowledge", press release, April 15th 2010

Baillie, D., presentation at *The Economist* Talent Management Summit, June 14th 2012

Heidrick & Struggles, *Mapping Global Talent – trends through 2012*, January 2010

Hill, J., "How firms define and execute talent strategy", *People Management* online, August 2012

Human Capital Institute (HCI), *What Influences Contract Talent Usage*, May 2011

Nooyi, I., presentation to Chief Executives Club of Boston, Boston College, Carroll School of Management, May 13th 2011

Ray, R.L. *et al.*, *False Summit: The State of Human Capital*, McKinsey/The Conference Board, 2012

"The workforce in the cloud", *The Economist*, June 1st 2013

3 Managing the talent process

"Age: a twenty-first century diversity imperative", Executive Case Report No. 4, Sloan Centre on Ageing and Work, Boston College, 2011

Barsh, J. and Lareina, Y., *Unlocking the Full Potential of Women At Work*, McKinsey & Co, 2012

Boeing's Workplace Innovation Lab – Engaging "Generation Y" as a powerful catalyst for productivity and change, Jonathan Winter, Career Innovation Company (Ci), October 15th 2010

Born, M. and Heers, M., *Talent Management: Alternatives to the Single-Ladder Approach*, report for EHRM (European Human Resource Management), July 2009

Carter, N. and Silva, C., *Pipeline's Broken Promise*, Catalyst, 2010

Caye, J. and Hinshaw, K., "Make talent, not war: serendipity to strategy", www.bcg.com, December 14th 2001

Economist Intelligence Unit, *Global Perspectives on Talent Management*, April 2011

Elop, S., Nokia internal memo, leaked on February 11th 2011

Hartley, D., "Raising global leaders at IBM", *Talent Management*, November 17th 2011

Korm, A. *et al.*, *Return on Leadership: Competencies that Generate Growth*, Egon Zehnder International and McKinsey & Co, February 2011

Nooyi, I., presentation to Chief Executives Club of Boston, Boston College, Carroll School of Management, May 13th 2011

Cover Story Interview: Sonali Roychowdhury, www.peoplematters.co.uk, August 23rd 2013

PriceWaterhouseCoopers, *Talent Mobility 2020: the Next Generation of International Assignments*, 2010

Reeves, M., *Adaptability: The New Competitive Advantage*, Boston Consulting Group, 2011

Sudhaker, B., presentation at *The Economist* Talent Management Summit, June 14th 2012

Syrett, M. and Devine, M., *Managing Uncertainty*, Profile Books, 2012

Talent and Enterprise Taskforce, *Tomorrow's Global Talent*, HM Government, February 2010

World Economic Forum, *Talent Mobility: Good Practices*, 2012

4 The individual and the organisation

Barsh, J. and Lareina, Y., *Unlocking the Full Potential of Women At Work*, McKinsey & Co, 2012

Cap Gemini, *The Talent Perspective: What does it feel like to be talent-managed?*, Chartered Institute of Personnel and Development, 2010

Carter, N. and Silva, C., *Mentoring: Necessary but Insufficient for Advancement*, Catalyst, 2010

Carter, N. and Silva, C., *Sponsoring Women to Success*, Catalyst, 2012

Devillard, S., Graven, W., Lawson, E., Paradise, R. and Sancier-Sultan, S., *Making the Breakthrough*, McKinsey & Co, 2012

Duran, A., Bartel, A. and Smith, A., *What Women Want in Business: A study of executives and entrepreneurs*, Korn/Ferry, 2001

Evans, R., presentation at *The Economist* Talent Management Summit, June 14th 2012

Hewlett, S.A. and Leader-Chivée, L., *Executive Presence*, Centre for Talent Innovation, November 2012

Honore, S. and Schofield, C.P., *Culture Shock: Generation Y and their managers*, Ashridge Business School, November 2012

Honore, S. and Schofield, C.P., *Generation Y: Inside Out*, Preliminary report (literature review), Ashridge Business School, 2009

Hornsey, L., presentation at *The Economist* Talent Management Summit, June 14th 2012

Ingham, J., presentation at *The Economist* Talent Management Summit, June 14th 2012

Institute of Leadership and Ashridge Business School, *Great Expectations: Managing Generation Y*, 2009.

Nooyi, I., presentation to Chief Executives Club of Boston, Boston College, Carroll School of Management, May 13th 2011

Pew Research Center, *Millennials: A Portrait of Generation Next*, February 2010

Robert Half International and Yahoo! Hotjobs, "Generation Y: what millennials really want", 2008

Sullivan, J., "Talent management lessons from Apple", www.ere.net, September 19th 2011

Tarnowski, L., presentation at *The Economist* Talent Management Summit, June 14th 2012

US Census Bureau, *Global Population Profile 2002*, Washington, DC

5 Taking a culture-led approach

AT&T Talent Network, case study, TMP Worldwide, September 7th 2010

Blass, E., *Maximising Talent for Business Performance*, Ashridge Research Group, 2007

Cullens, J., presentation at *The Economist* Talent Management Summit, June 14th 2012

Cap Gemini, *The Talent Perspective: What does it feel like to be talent-managed?*, Chartered Institute of Personnel and Development, 2010

Clear/M&C Saatchi, *Top 20 Desirable Brands in the UK 2013*

Hornsey, L., presentation at *The Economist* Talent Management Summit, June 14th 2012

Original research drawn from Narasimhan, A. and Dogra, A.M., "Hiring and retention at Naukri", *Financial Times*, April 23rd 2012

Nooyi, I., presentation to Chief Executives Club of Boston, Boston College, Carroll School of Management, May 13th 2011

Sudhaker, B., presentation at *The Economist* Talent Management Summit, June 14th 2012

6 Creating a talent eco-system

Dehnugara, K., presentation at *The Economist* Talent Management Summit, June 14th 2012

Leighton, P. et al., *Working as an Independent Professional (IPro) in the EU: Seeking the Success Factors*, European Forum of Independent Professionals, 2013

Sinetar, M., "Entrepreneurs, Chaos and Creativity: Can Creative People Survive Large Company Structures?", *Sloan Management Review*, winter 1985

7 Playing the talent game

Armstrong, C., "Going on secondment", Jobs.ac.uk, July 2007

Baillie, D., presentation at *The Economist* Talent Management Summit, June 14th 2012

Clawson, T., "Please mind the gap", *Director*, July 2007

Hornsey, L., presentation at *The Economist* Talent Management Summit, June 14th 2012

Khurana, N., presentation at *The Economist* Talent Management Summit, June 14th 2012

Leighton, P. *et al.*, *Working as an Independent Professional (IPro) in the EU: Seeking the Success Factors*, European Forum of Independent Professionals, 2013

Nooyi, I., presentation to Chief Executives Club of Boston, Boston College, Carroll School of Management, May 13th 2011

8 Planning for the future

Chatman, J. *et al.*, "Case-study: Cisco Systems", *Financial Times*, June 15th 2011

Evans, R., presentation at *The Economist* Talent Management Summit, June 14th 2012

Michaels, E., Handfield-Jones, H. and Axelrod, B., *The War for Talent*, Harvard Business School Press, 2001

Index